Slow Dance on the
Killing Ground

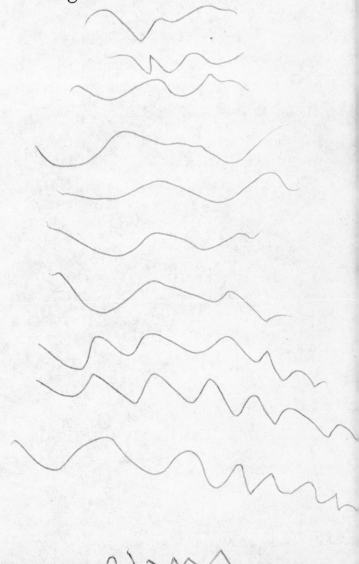

SLOW

DANCE *on*

the KILLING

GROUND

* *
*

A Play by

William Hanley

Random House
New York

23502

PHOTOS COURTESY OF FRIEDMAN—ABELES

MANUFACTURED IN THE UNITED STATES OF AMERICA

IN MEMORIAM

Panos Kyrtsis

17 May 1934 — 12 September 1963

SLOW DANCE ON THE KILLING GROUND *was first presented by Hume Cronyn, Allen-Hodgdon, Inc., Stevens Productions, Inc., and Bonfils-Seawell Enterprises at the Plymouth Theatre on November 30, 1964, with the following cast:*

GLAS	George Rose
RANDALL	Clarence Williams
ROSIE	Carolan Daniels

Directed by Joseph Anthony

Production designed by Oliver Smith

Costumes by Ann Roth

Lighting by Jack Brown

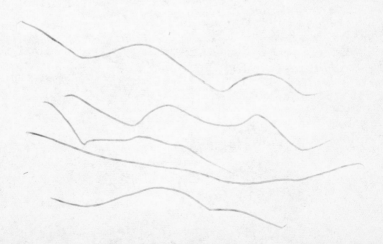

The play happens on the night of June 1, 1962, in a small store in a district of warehouses and factories in Brooklyn, and in the kitchen of the apartment adjoining the store. In the surrounding streets the buildings are squat and dark, the street lamps unlit. Viewed from a distance, the dim glow cast into the street through the window of the lighted store would be seen to be the only light in a great, stone darkness.

But for a lapse of some five minutes or so between the first and second scenes of Act Two, the action is continuous.

Act One

Pas de Deux

ACT ONE

The shop is the kind of place usually referred to in New York City as a candy store, but whose merchandise and function cover a much wider range in service and activity than that term would suggest.

The entrance to the store is in the center wall. To the right of this door there is a very large plate-glass window, unwashed and clouded. Below the window, and running parallel to the upper wall, is the counter-top of a soda fountain, in front of which are several wooden stools. To the left of the street entrance, upstage, there is a single small table with chairs. Part of the right wall, to a height of six feet or so from the floor, is covered with racks for magazines and garish paperbound books. In front of these racks is a low bench for the display of newspapers; above the racks, too high to reach without the aid of a ladder, there are glass-fronted cabinets, crammed with a miscellany of merchandise: most everything from shaving supplies to stationery. Against the left wall, downstage, there is a juke box, glitteringly new, in jarring conflict with its surroundings. Near the juke box there is a wall telephone. In the right wall an open doorway gives access to a dimly lit hallway which leads to the kitchen. The kitchen occupies the far right of the stage and is unlit now. The store is lit with a number of hanging lightbulbs covered with conical green metal shades.

It is a moment before GLAS enters, through the doorway at the right, carrying an eight-foot stepladder on his shoulder. GLAS is a man of sixty-five, slow of movement, but with an intimation of strength about him. His very erect *bearing is marred only by a mild but very definite limp. He is an unusually alert and observant man but a silent one by nature; so that, although he absorbs all that goes on about him, he does not ordinarily feel compelled to comment upon it.*

He opens the legs of the ladder and settles them in front of the magazine racks. He ascends the ladder and opens the door of one of the glass-fronted cabinets: the ladder has been badly placed, however, and now the cabinet door jars against the top of the ladder and will not open fully. He reacts not at all to this, only closes the door, descends the ladder, moves it to the left, ascends the ladder and opens the cabinet door to its fullest. He thoughtfully regards the contents of the cabinet, descends the ladder and moves to the rear of the soda fountain. He stoops, is out of sight for a moment, then reappears holding a large ledger and a clipboard, to which are fastened several sheets of paper. He places these on the counter-top and moves around the counter. He opens the ledger, finds the page, returns to the ladder and ascends it. He removes a box from the cabinet, counts its contents, descends the ladder and makes a notation on the inventory sheet attached to the clipboard. He ascends the ladder again and is in the process of counting the contents of a second box when the door is jolted open and RANDALL *bounds in from the street.*

RANDALL *is a Negro boy of eighteen, slim, wiry, handsome. He is wearing a close-fitting suit with a somewhat short jacket and velvet collar, a narrow-brimmed hat with a high crown, and a rather voluminous cape that falls to his hips. He carries a tightly rolled umbrella. The over-all effect is somewhat Edwardian but for the dirty white sneakers on his feet and the dark glasses he wears.*

4

At the sound of his entrance, GLAS *has turned, unseen by* RANDALL, *to watch the boy.* RANDALL *is breathless, as from a long run, and highly agitated. He closes the door behind him and rests his back upon it. He looks about quickly and believes the place to be deserted. After a moment, he calms and relaxes, but even then his movements are relatively quick and tense. Throughout, he has been humming a tune, quietly, absently. He looks quickly about the place and takes only a single step before* GLAS *speaks.*

GLAS   So?
    (RANDALL *starts, almost violently, and it is a moment, a split second, before he discovers* GLAS *atop the ladder. His demeanor changes instantly to an attitude of breeziness, near gaiety*)

RANDALL   Hey, daddy! (GLAS *merely gazes, silent*) Didn't see you up there! Pretty neat, yes indeedy!

GLAS   Neat?

RANDALL   I mean, you pretty much able to keep your eye on matters from up there, right? Panoramic view. Pan-o-ramic! Neat.

GLAS (*Confused, gesturing with the box*)   No, I'm only—

RANDALL   Man! It's hot, ain't it?

GLAS (*Descending the ladder*)   What can I do for you?

RANDALL   Oh, well now! That there's a question, ain't it!

GLAS   What?

RANDALL   I mean, what can you *do* for me. The possibilities are endless, know what I mean? Right? But we start with somethin' easy. Gimme a . . . gimme an egg cream.

5

GLAS (*Starting for the rear of the counter*) Chocolate?

RANDALL That's a nice flavor.

GLAS (*Halts abruptly, remembering*) I can't.

RANDALL Can't what?

GLAS Make an egg cream. My seltzer water, the tap's broken.

RANDALL Now, ain't that the way? Ain't that always the way? You ask me what can you do for me, I give you somethin' real easy to start with and you got a busted tap on your seltzer water. Man, oh, man. How you fixed for a bottle of lemon soda, say?

GLAS Lemon soda I got.

RANDALL Crazy. (GLAS *takes the soda from the freezer behind the counter, removes the cap and gives the bottle to* RANDALL) You open kinda late, ain'tcha?

GLAS I don't know.

RANDALL You don't know?

GLAS What time is it?

RANDALL 'Cordin' to my twenny-one jewel, Swiss movement chronometer calendar watch it now six minutes after ten o'clock P.M., June the first, nineteen sixty-two.

GLAS Yes.

RANDALL Hmm?

GLAS Yes, I'm open late.
(GLAS *moves from behind the counter to resume his inventory and is constantly ascending and descending the ladder throughout what follows, while* RAN-

DALL, *nervous, peering out the window and the door, is moving always. He hums again for a moment the same tune*)

RANDALL   How *come* you open so late?

GLAS   Why not?

RANDALL   I mean, it ain't so safe around here so late. You ain't afraid of gettin' robbed or nothin' like that?
(*There is a pause while* GLAS *regards the store*)

GLAS   What's to steal?

RANDALL   (*Laughs shortly*)   Yeah, well, I see what you mean: you ain't goin' to exactly get no Good House-keepin' Seal of Approval. About what time you figurin' on closin' up? I mean, approximate?

GLAS   Oh . . . sooner or later. No hurry.

RANDALL   Well, what I mean, you gotta go to *sleep* sometime, right?

GLAS   I don't sleep much.

RANDALL   Oh, that right?

GLAS   I don't like to sleep.
(*From the street, footsteps are heard on the pavement, approaching. Almost imperceptibly,* RANDALL *tenses and becomes still. This is seen by* GLAS, *but* RANDALL *is unaware of being observed: the footsteps, it seems, are more important. The steps grow louder and pass by.* RANDALL's *attention is still on the street when he speaks again*)

RANDALL   Why's that.

GLAS   Hm?

RANDALL (*Turning to* GLAS) That you don't like to sleep. (*Pause*)

GLAS I dream.

RANDLL Yeah...?

GLAS (*Absently*) Mm.
(RANDALL *waits, expecting some elaboration, but after a silence,* GLAS *resumes his work.* RANDALL'*s attention begins now, slowly, to focus more on* GLAS, *less on the street*)

RANDALL You of European abstraction.

GLAS I beg your pardon?

RANDALL Your accent. Originally you speak another tongue, I mean, you come from across the sea, right?

GLAS Oh. *Extraction.*

RANDALL Sir?

GLAS You said *ab*straction. The word is *ex*traction. European *ex*traction.

RANDALL Oh. Yeah . . . Well, I stand corrected, daddy.

GLAS (*Definitely, pressing the point*) Extraction.

RANDALL You the precise type, I be sure to watch my step with you—linguistically speakin'. (RANDALL *prowls for a moment, moves to the door, peers out into the darkness. He sings quietly to himself; the tune is recognizable as the one he has been humming*) "I went to the rock to hide my face/ The rock cried out, no hiding place . . ." (*Pause*) You know there ain't a single light out there at all? For about twenny blocks? I mean, the street lights, daddy, they all *out!*

GLAS   Repairing the power lines. They've been digging up the street for about two weeks now.

RANDALL   Well, dig they must, daddy, dig they must. This is a kinda kooky place for a store though, ain't it.

GLAS   Why.

RANDALL   Well, I mean, it is what you might say, off the beaten track, somewhat removed from the bustling lanes of commerce.

GLAS   Only at night. In the daytime I do okay with the factory people. At night it's quiet. I like it that way.

RANDALL   You ain't afraid to go home this late at night?

GLAS   You ask a lot of questions, sonny.

RANDALL   Well, it's just that I'm of the inquirin' type of mind. No offense intended, I hasten to assure you, sir.
   (*There is a pause, during which* GLAS *studies* RANDALL *and mistakenly interprets his answer to be sincere*)

GLAS   This is home. (*Pointing*) In the back.

RANDALL   Crazy.

GLAS   What's crazy about it?

RANDALL   No, there do seem to be some misunderstandin' here this evenin'. Crazy: that means, uh . . . that's all right, that's good.

GLAS   What's all right?

RANDALL   That you *live* here, daddy. I mean, it is an *excellent i-dea!*

GLAS   Ah.

9

RANDALL   You'll see: pretty soon we be understandin' each other perfect. You mind if I ask you another little question? One which might prove to be to your definite benefit?

GLAS   Mm?

RANDALL   You climb up to the top of that there ladder, right? Then you count the stuff in one a them boxes, right? Then you climb down the ladder and write on that there paper, right?

GLAS   Inventory, yeah.

RANDALL   Yeah, but it'd be a lot faster you took the paper up there on the ladder.
  (*Pause*)

GLAS   What's the hurry?

RANDALL   Oh. Well, now, you got a point there. Long as you ain't in no hurry.

GLAS   I don't see you around here before, sonny.

RANDALL   You like to do me a little favor?

GLAS   What.

RANDALL   Don't call me sonny.

GLAS   What's your name?

RANDALL (*After a pause*)   Why.

GLAS (*Obviously*)   You don't want me to call you sonny, what should I call you?

RANDALL   Winston.

GLAS   Winston. Okay.

RANDALL   Winston Churchill.
   (*Pause*)

GLAS   This is a joke?

RANDALL   You don't think I look like my name could be
   Winston Churchill?

GLAS   It makes no difference to me one way or the other.

RANDALL   Tell you the truth, my name is Franz . . . Franz
   Kafka.
   (*Pause*)

GLAS   You should be on the TV with your funny line of
   jokes—sonny.

RANDALL   You know Franz Kafka? I don't mean did you
   know him personally, I mean you know who he was?
   (*No response*) You know that story he write where this
   fella wake up one mornin' and find out he turned into
   a *bug*? You know that story? That actually happen to
   me.

GLAS (*Drily*)   Is that right.

RANDALL   Yeah. One mornin' I wake up and I realize I'm
   actually a *bug*. I *look* the same, like always, you know,
   but actually I'm a *bug*.

GLAS   How is that.

RANDALL   Oh well, it a little too complicated to explain
   just at the present moment. Some other time, maybe.

GLAS   Don't you ever stand still, boy?

RANDALL   Stand still! Baby, get *me* to stand still they
   gonna have to nail my feet to the floor! *To the floor!*
   (*He hurls his umbrella, like a spear, at the floor. The*

*stem, apparently sharpened to a point, pierces the wood
and the umbrella stands by itself)* Know what I mean?
*(He retrieves the umbrella and cleans the point
caressingly in the palm of his hand)*

GLAS That's dangerous.

RANDALL Ain't it now? You know I got a IQ of a hundred and eighty-seven? Yeah. A hundred and eighty-
seven. Fact.

GLAS *(Smiling)* Oh, yeah?

RANDALL Yeah, that the reaction that information usually
get. It a true statement, nevertheless. Eighteen years
old and a IQ of a hundred and eighty-seven. When I
was a little kid they used to be always givin' me a lotta
these here tests, you know? They take me up to Colum-
bia University and all these cats be sittin' around puffin'
on their pipes and askin' me a lotta questions, you know,
tryin' to figure out how it could happen I be so smart.
But that's just the way it is: a genius is what I am. I got
a photographic memory, you know? Sometimes known
as total recall. That's where you read somethin' just once
and you remember the whole thing, every word. You
know? Like for instance, would you care to hear me
quote some of the book *War and Peace* by Count Leo
Tolstoy? I could quote you some a that now if you was
a mind to hear it. I couldn't quote you nothin' past page
one hundred and forty-six, though, 'cause that's as far
as I got in that particular book, it actually a rather borin'
book, if you know what I mean. (GLAS *smiles*) What's
so amusin'?

GLAS It happens to be one of the greatest books.

RANDALL   Yeah, I heard that. Bored the shit outta *me*.

GLAS   When you get older you'll be able to appreciate it.

RANDALL   You think so, uh? (GLAS *nods*) You read that book, then, uh?

GLAS   Mm.

RANDALL   Mm. So anyway, here I am with this here fantastic IQ, you see what I mean? Of course, as is clear and apparent to the naked eye, I am, withal, a young gentleman of some color—which limits my horizons considerable in this here present society we got, notwithstandin' IQ's and all.

GLAS   Not necessarily. If you're as smart as you say, you could do great things.

RANDALL   For my race?

GLAS   What?

RANDALL   That's what they used to be tellin' me all the time when I was on the inside. With a mind like you got, Randall, you could be doin' great things for your race. Unquote.

GLAS   Inside where?

RANDALL   Oh, you know: a reform school here, a co-rectional institution there, a work farm for minor offenders upstate I was on for a while, *that* was very nice, lots a fresh air, you know? They was always sayin' that: with a mind like you got, Randall, you could be doin' great things for your race. It never occurred to them to say I could be doin' great things for *me*. Not that I got a mind to do that neither, but it woulda been a nice change from all that jazz about great things for my race, if you know what I mean. You probably find it hard to believe, but havin' a IQ of a hundred and eighty-seven is actually rather borin'. My name is Randall. I mean, that my true name. 'Cause I don't want you callin' me sonny or boy or nothin' like that. Okay? Randall . . . Okay?

GLAS Okay.

RANDALL I actually *was* Winston there for a while some time back. Also Franz for a bit. It all depend what I'm feelin' like any particular time. Last time I was Randall was for about a week or so a couple months ago so this time it what you might say a return engagement by popular demand. I don't know who I be next. Maybe Maximilian. I been readin' a book here about him. (*From a pocket within the cape he takes out a small book*) He was the Emperor of Mexico for a little bit there some time back, you know. Man! What wouldn't it be like to be an emperor. An emperor! . . . Even if you did get your ass shot off in the end. Yeah, I think maybe I be Maximilian next time. What's yours?

GLAS What?

RANDALL Your name, I mean.

(GLAS *gazes at him for a moment before answering*)

GLAS Glas.

RANDALL Glass?

GLAS With one s.

RANDALL What kinda name is that, Glas with one s?

GLAS German for the Glas with two esses.

RANDALL Oh, I dig. German. (*Points to the window*) Glass with two esses. (*Points to* GLAS) Glas with one s.

Neat. Short and sweet. Actually, that other s is entirely unnecessary anyway, right? I mean, it just kinda dangle there, doin' nothin'. Like, the point is already made by the time one gets to the first s, right? I like that: Glas with one s. And now that my attention been called to it, and you don't mind me sayin', but the glass with two esses here could use a little washin', I do believe.

GLAS   Why.

RANDALL   Why! Well, daddy, you can't hardly even see *through* it. It downright *dirty*, that glass with two esses.

GLAS   There's nothing out there I particularly want to see.

RANDALL   Is that right?

GLAS   That's right.

RANDALL   You don't like the nature of things out there particularly?

GLAS   Exactly.

RANDALL   Well now, you see? I had a feelin', I just *knew* we was brothers under the skin, somehow. I hasten to repeat, *under* the skin, no offense intended, no indeed, sir. But I know exactly what you mean, exactly! I mean, it is grotesque out there, ain't it, now? It is . . . *bizarre!* You know what that is out there, daddy? You know? That is the *killing* ground out there.

GLAS   The what?

RANDALL   I mean that's no man's land out there, daddy! That somebody *else's* turf, a regular *mine field*, you gotta step *care*fully, they *kill* you out there, know what I mean?

15

GLAS Not exactly.

RANDALL Butcher shop. It a regular butcher shop out there. You know what happened out there just last year alone?

GLAS Do I know what *happened*?

RANDALL Just last year alone.

GLAS What happened?

RANDALL What happened out there—and I quote—what happened out there was four hundred and eighty-three homicides! (*He becomes completely still for the first time since his entrance, closes his eyes and recites, from memory*) "Contrary to public impression, most homicides are spontaneous and are committed in the home; they are not the result of gangland reprisals but of family disputes. These facts about murder were revealed today by Police Commissioner Michael J. Murphy in releasing a report by his department's Statistical and Records Bureau in a dossier of such crimes during 1961. Out of four hundred and eighty-three homicides last year, an increase of ninety-three over the preceding year, eighty-seven and four-tenths percent were solved or cleared by arrests. A study of them discloses the following: fifty-three percent of the homicides occurred between seven P.M. and three A.M.; three hundred and ninety-seven of the victims were over twenty-one; thirty-four were under seven. One hundred and thirteen of the victims were women; ninety-eight women were arrested for homicide. Two hundred and six (forty-two and seven-tenths percent) occurred in homes; one hundred and twenty-nine (twenty-six and seven-tenths percent) occurred on the street. Thirty-five occurred in hallways; sixteen occurred in bars and grills. Two hundred and forty-nine homicides resulted from altercations; fifty-nine from family squabbles; twenty-five from apparent robberies; twenty-two (four and six-tenths percent of all cases) were committed by heroin users. Knives and other sharp instruments were used in forty-three percent. Revolvers and rifles were used in twenty and three-tenths percent. Physical force accounted for eighteen percent. Seven were the result of teenage gang conflicts (all in Brooklyn). Two hundred and thirty-nine were committed in Manhattan. One hundred and fifty were committed in Brooklyn. Sixty in the Bronx. Twenty-nine in Queens. Five in Richmond. Fifteen husbands were slain by their wives. Eighteen wives were slain by their husbands . . . ten sons were slain by their mothers . . . two sons were slain by their fathers . . . six daughters were slain by their mothers . . . four daughters were slain by their fathers . . . one father was killed by his daughter . . . two mothers were killed by their sons . . . four stepfathers were killed by their stepsons . . . one stepfather was killed by his stepdaughter . . . two sisters killed their brothers . . . three brothers killed their brothers . . . one son-in-law killed his father-in-law . . . one father-in-law killed his son-in-law . . . one son-in-law killed his mother-in-law . . . one despondent mother drowned her three children in the East River . . . another despondent mother drowned her three children in a bathtub . . . one child was killed for bedwetting . . ." (*Pause*) Oh, man, man . . .

> (*There is a long silence.* GLAS *appears to be quite absorbed in the recitation.* RANDALL *seems not to be*

present at all. For a moment or so the sound of an approaching truck is heard; it slows outside the store and there is the sound of two heavy thumps on the sidewalk. The sound brings GLAS *and* RANDALL *out of their immobility:* RANDALL *starts and becomes alerted, an action that does not go unnoticed by* GLAS *as he moves toward the door. The truck pulls away loudly.* GLAS *opens the door and exits.* RANDALL *waits, tensed, until* GLAS *re-enters carrying two bundles of tabloid newspapers tied with heavy cord)*

GLAS   I've been meaning to ask you something.

RANDALL   Yeah?

GLAS   About your eyes.

RANDALL   What about 'em?

GLAS   Is there something wrong with them?

RANDALL   Ain't nothin' wrong with my eyes.

GLAS   Oh.
(*He has cut the cord on one of the bundles and taken up the top newspaper; he peruses the front page. for a moment—a huge headline—emits a non-committal grunt and tosses the paper aside on the counter-top. The remaining newspapers he begins to arrange on the bench in front of the magazine rack)*

RANDALL   What makes you think there somethin' wrong with my eyes?

GLAS   I wondered why you wear sunglasses in the middle of the night.

RANDALL   Oh. Well, I like 'em. *You* know.

18

GLAS Ah.

RANDALL Bet you thought there was gonna be some complicated and interestin' reason why I was wearin' shades in the middle of the night, hah? No, it's just that I like 'em, you know?

GLAS Ah.

RANDALL Except maybe it's because I like the nighttime and sometimes it ain't nighttime enough . . . Know what I mean?

GLAS (*After a moment*) Yes.

RANDALL No, you don't.

GLAS What?

RANDALL You don't know what I mean. Man, don't say you know what I mean if you don't know what I mean.

GLAS (*Angrily*) I know what you mean!

RANDALL Oh, now, maaan. Don't be that way. Hot night like this here, we gotta remain calm, we gotta maintain a cool view toward matters in general, right? (*He takes up the newspaper from the counter; offhandedly*) I see where they really hung his ass, hah? (*No response from* GLAS *save a stare*) This here Nazi cat, I mean. Them Jews really hung his ass, *after* all. How you pronounce that name?

(GLAS *turns away to resume his work.*)

GLAS Eichmann.

RANDALL (*Reproducing the sound with precision*) Eichmann. Adolf Eichmann. Them German names gimme a lotta trouble. German and Russian, they very tough to

19

pronounce. I do very good with the French, though. Baudelaire. That's a French name. (*And, more carefully, savoring it*) Baudelaire . . . I guess you know he was one a them French poets. Why you figure they done that, anyway?

GLAS What?

RANDALL The Jews. Why you figure they hung this here Eichmann chap?

GLAS Look, sonny—

RANDALL Oh, now, Mister Glas, sir, there you go *again*. *Sonny*. What is it, you don't like to get on a first-name basis with, uh—certain types, shall we say?

GLAS What do you mean, certain types?

RANDALL You know what I mean. I mean me bein' a young gentleman of some color.

GLAS Sonny, I don't care if you'd be purple with orange stripes.

RANDALL Oh, now, *that's* a clashy combination. Tha's all we'd need, things ain't tough enough.

GLAS Yeah, sure.

RANDALL I do perceive you ain't got much sympathy for some a the various and sundry dilemmas currently facin' mankind, then?

GLAS I stay right here and I watch the world go by and I don't get in its way.

RANDALL Yeah, but you can't do that, daddy.

GLAS Why not.

RANDALL   Because ... well ... because you can't.

GLAS   You're a genius, you can't think of a better reason than that?

RANDALL   Well, what I mean, because sooner or later it gonna come walkin' right in that door there. With a gun in its hand or somethin' maybe.

GLAS   What?

RANDALL   Well, that just a figure of speech. What I mean, the whole world got a gun in its hand. Like what I was sayin' before. You see what I mean atall? (*Pause*) Yeah, I see you see what I mean.

GLAS   In that case I got one too. (*He reaches beneath the counter and comes up with a revolver in his hand*) Hah? (*Pause*)

RANDALL   (*Quietly*)   Well now, well now. I thought you wasn't a member of the club, you been sayin'. You a member in good standin', dues all paid up.

GLAS   No. (*He returns the gun to its place beneath the counter*)

RANDALL   Oh, come on now, daddy, *I* dig. You got yours, I got mine. (*He hurls the umbrella at the floor again*) We prepared!

GLAS   No.
      (RANDALL *retrieves the umbrella and points it at* GLAS *like a rifle*)

RANDALL   Bang!
      (*Pause. They gaze, taking each other's measure*)

GLAS   What were you running away from?

RANDALL Sir?

GLAS When you came in here: what were you running away from?

RANDALL Where'd you get an idea like that, baby? Where in the world?

GLAS I'll give you some advice.

RANDALL Oh, boy.

GLAS You got trouble out there, don't bring it in here. (GLAS *comes from behind the counter with a feather duster in his hand*)

RANDALL You barkin' up the incorrect tree, daddy.

GLAS I got the right tree, all right.
(*He ascends the ladder*)

RANDALL Your mistake is in a definite misinterpretation of my basic approach. You see? What I mean, that just the manner in which I happen to come on: like gangbusters.

GLAS I don't know what you're talking about, the way you talk, I'm just telling you—

RANDALL You don't understand?

GLAS I'm just telling you—

RANDALL Which part?

GLAS What?

RANDALL Which part? I mean, which portion of my previous statements there don't you understand? I be glad to explain it to you in more detail.
(*Pause*)

GLAS (*Quietly*) Maybe you better leave now, hah?

RANDALL Leave? *Leave?*

GLAS Out.

RANDALL What is it you got against me, anyway?

GLAS Out.

RANDALL You prejudiced, ain'tcha.

GLAS Out.

RANDALL Actually, I seen it right the minute I come in the door. We can always tell, you know. Always tell.

GLAS (*Testily*) Tell what!

RANDALL (*Smiling, conspiratorial*) You know.

GLAS Now look, sonny, I already told—

RANDALL Like that: see what I mean? You absolutely and categorically refuse to address me by my proper and true name. Little things like that, see what I mean? Little things like that's how we can always tell. Sonny. Boy. Little things like that. I guess you be prejudiced against the Jews, too, if you wasn't one yourself. (*Silence.* GLAS *smiles; the smile broadens and ends in a short laugh*) Yeah, actually that was a very amusin' remark, I suppose.

GLAS What makes you think I'm a Jew?

RANDALL There's ways, daddy.

GLAS What ways?

RANDALL Well, I mean, I ain't exactly stupid, you know? I ain't exactly *un-in-telligent*. I think you forgettin' my IQ that I was tellin' you about a bit ago there.

GLAS One hundred eighty-seven.

RANDALL Right.

GLAS Nevertheless, I'm not a Jew. (RANDALL *smiles*) Why don't you believe me?

RANDALL Well, man, if there's one thing I can tell right off when I see one, it's a Jew.

GLAS Oh?

RANDALL Sure.

GLAS That's very interesting.

RANDALL Oh, yeah.

GLAS How.

RANDALL Mm?

GLAS How do you go about it?

RANDALL Oh, well, man, it a little too subtle and complicated to go into just at the present moment.

GLAS You said that before.

RANDALL Said what before?

GLAS What you just said: that it's too complicated to explain.

RANDALL No, man, we ain't been talkin' about Jews before just now.

GLAS You said it about something else.

24

RANDALL Oh, yeah? What'd I say it about, Mister Glas, sir?

GLAS When you said you were a bug.

RANDALL Oh. Yeah. Truly.

GLAS Why did you say that?

RANDALL That I'm a bug? (GLAS *nods*) Because I am. We all are.

GLAS Who.

RANDALL All of us. We are *all* bugs. You, me. Everybody! Everywhere!

GLAS Bugs.

RANDALL Sure. Just waitin' to be squashed.

GLAS By whom?

RANDALL Bigger bugs. You see, baby, what is euphimistly called life is actually just one big bug house and you either gotta—

GLAS Euphemistically.

RANDALL What'd I say?

GLAS Euphimistly. What—?

RANDALL Euphemistically. Oh. Actually, you bein' very helpful to fillin' in the small gaps in my education. Where was I? Oh, yeah. So you either gotta grow up to be one a them big bugs or you gotta scurry. Know

what I mean? *Scurry.* You stand still and you find yourself bein' *squashed.* That one of my philosophies of life.
What's one of yours?

GLAS   What?

RANDALL   Philosophies of life.

GLAS   I have none.
(*He turns his attention to the cabinet, his back to*
RANDALL)

RANDALL   Sure you do, you already told me one. You said
to me, you said, uh . . . *you* know, that you was gonna
cool it right in here and you wasn't gettin' in nobody's
way. That's one philosophy of life, but I mean, what's
another one of your favorites?

GLAS (*Amused*)   I have to have more than one?

RANDALL   Oh, well, man, certainly! (*While he speaks,*
RANDALL *quickly and quietly gropes behind the counter*
and comes up with the gun in his hand; it disappears
into a pocket within the cape) I mean, you got only one
philosophy of life and then the situation changes, *then*
where are you? Know what I mean? I mean, you gotta
have several diverse philosophies to operate on, dependin'
on the various situations that you find yourself meetin'
up with. (*Pause.* GLAS *gazes a moment, shakes his head,*
smiling, and descends the ladder) Am I botherin' you?

GLAS (*Equably*)   No.

RANDALL   Actually, you ain't of the opinion that I'm even
worth botherin' *about,* right?

GLAS   Why do you say that?

RANDALL   Well, I mean, baby, you ain't exactly *respondin'* to me, know what I mean? I mean, here I go and present in a polite and intelligent manner of speakin' a certain opinion that I gone to a lotta trouble to, uh—formulate. And you don't respond *atall*. All you do, you sorta *smiiile* there and go right on about your business. Your attitude is that I'm more or less beneath your attention, right?

GLAS   Aren't you hot with all them clothes on?

RANDALL   I don't sweat, it's a peculiarity I got. (*He takes an apple from a pocket within the cape, bites into it*) What'd you have in mind I was runnin' away from?

GLAS   How would I know?

RANDALL   True. 'Course there's a lotta possibilities. I guess you already considered to yourself privately some of the possibilities of what I mighta been runnin' away from. If I *was* runnin' away. Lemme see, now . . . Could be I knocked over my friendly neighborhood grocery store to get me an apple and a little loose change? . . . Or perhaps I am a remnant of one of our local altercations commonly known as the gang rumble, in which several children have been left slain, slain on the field of battle? . . . That don't appeal to you, neither? Well, lemme see, now . . . Could be I just recently committed a criminal assault on a white lady of middle age in the dark and deserted end of a subway station platform? . . . No? . . . Or perhaps, *perhaps*—this a good one—perhaps I just up and done away with my momma, stabbin' her numerous times about the breast and abdomen with a ice pick.
    (*From within the cape, an ice pick appears in his hand; he drives it into the counter-top. Pause*)

27

GLAS   You could be arrested for having a thing like that.

RANDALL   I could be arrested for jaywalkin'. It all relative, know what I mean?

GLAS   What are you doing with such a thing?

RANDALL   Well . . . you can't never tell when I'm gonna run into a block of ice. Like I was sayin' earlier on, I like to be prepared for all and sundry eventualities. Looked upon in a certain way, and dependin' on the use to which it is put, a ice pick is also a philosophy of life. Never fear, however: you can be certain that if I committed one a them depredations just enumerated, you can be certain that sooner or later the sword of justice will pierce my heart. Sooner or later. Actually, as a matter of fact, I am the possessor of a rather *unique* and *original* type of heart, but I save that to tell you about for some other time. (*He returns the ice pick to a pocket within the cape*) You really a Jew, then, right?
        (*Pause*)

GLAS   Why.

RANDALL   'Cause if you a Jew, I was just wonderin' so what do you think about that, then.

GLAS   About what.

RANDALL   This here Mister Adolf Eichmann swingin' gently in the mornin' breeze.

GLAS   I don't think anything about it.

RANDALL   Well, daddy, you must think *somethin'* about it.

GLAS   Why.

RANDALL   Well, I mean, man, send not to know for whom the chap swings, he swings for thee, you know?

GLAS Thee? Who.

RANDALL *You* chaps. The Jews.

GLAS You think so?

RANDALL That the impression under which I been laborin' these here many months.
(*Pause*)

GLAS What were you running away from?
(*Pause*)

RANDALL You the persistent type, though, ain't you, daddy. Ain't always a good idea to be too persistent, though, you know? . . . I mean, "What is Truth?' said Jesting Pilate and would not stay for an answer." You know who said that? You know? (*No response from* GLAS) Francis Bacon was the one who said that. Would you care for me to tell you about my unique and original type of heart?

GLAS What about it.

RANDALL Got a hole in it.
(RANDALL *has taken a handful of wooden kitchen matches from his pocket and strikes one now, holding it up before him, regarding the flame*)

GLAS A hole?

RANDALL Born like that, a little old hole in my heart.

GLAS (*Drily*) That certainly is a unique and original type of heart.

RANDALL It is my private theory that this interesting condition of my heart had somethin' to do with the fact of me bein' born durin' a partial eclipse of the sun.

29

GLAS   An eclipse of the sun.

RANDALL   *Partial* eclipse, *partial.* (Strikes another match) I mean, I detect and suspect a somewhat remote and abstrac' relationship 'tween the two facts of me bein' born with a hole in my heart *and* durin' a partial *eclipse* of the sun. 'Course there is no substantiation for that theory as yet. But I'm workin' on it all the time. 'M I confusin' you?

GLAS   No, no.

RANDALL   You lookin' at me in a very puzzled tone of voice. You probably thinkin' it a lotta shit about me bein' born with a hole in my heart durin' a partial *eclipse* of the sun, right? I admit it sound unlikely in the extreme. But when you stop for a just a bitty minute and think about it, *everything* sound unlikely the first time around, know what I mean? I mean, take for an example a simple thing like, uh—fire. Like, the very first time, way back there, when one chap said to another chap, Hey, Charlie, looky here! We *got* us a *fire!* Now, don't you know that other chap look at him somewhat *askance* and say, Oh, well now, *that* very unlikely, ain't it? Don't you know? (GLAS *stares.* RANDALL *lights another match*) Doubting Thomas . . . I'd let you stick your finger in *my* wound, 'cept it be somewhat difficult.

GLAS   What are you supposed to be, the Statue of Liberty, or what.

RANDALL   Fire, daddy, fire! Hot!

GLAS   (*Taking in the store*)   Look, sonny, it ain't much, but I like it. So stop with the matches.

RANDALL (*A caricature*) Yassah, boss, yassah! Tote that barge! Lift that bale! Git a little drunk and they hang you on a nail! If you're *white*, you're *right*! Shuffle, shuffle, shuffle!

GLAS I don't like that kind of talk.

RANDALL What kinda talk is that, daddy?

GLAS And stop calling me daddy.

RANDALL No offense intended, sir, I assure you. It is definitely not my intention to impugn the purity of your ancestral heritage, and I quite understand and sympathize with your objections, seein' as how I heard that a lotta you German folks was unusually sensitive to that topic at one time in the not-too-distant past. 'Course, you bein' a Jew and all I been inclined to think of you bein' somewhat *less* sensitive in that there area. But I stand corrected, definitely, sir.

GLAS I'm not a Jew.

RANDALL You ain't?

GLAS No.

RANDALL Well now, I was definitely under the impression that you'd give me to understand—

GLAS Sonny, why don't you go home now.

RANDALL I'm already there, baby.

GLAS Oh? Your trunks are arriving later?

RANDALL Oh-oh, there you go again, slashin' away at me with your biting and satirical wit. No, but what I mean, where I *am* is home. Any particular place I happen to find myself, that's home. My walls are the space around me and heaven is my roof. Poetic like that. I live in my skin, baby, like everyone else. "I am black, but, oh, my soul is white." You know who said that? William Blake said that. He was a poet too. But I can see I ain't makin' myself quite as clear as I might oughtta be doin'. The point is, that home, like in the conventional sense of the term as you are usin' it, I got none. I just move, baby, move. Here, there, everywhere.

GLAS   I suppose you sleepwalking around too, hah?

RANDALL   Oh, well, no, baby, I ain't quite perfected my organism to that level of development as yet. Of course, I got certain physical requirements that requires me to grab forty, fifty winks now and again. But there's lots a places for that if one is smart and uses the natural intelligence. For instance, I can always go down into the subway and get me the local to Pelham Bay Park and back again, which take about three days, sleepin' all the way. 'Course I'm exaggeratin' there about the three days, but if you was to do it with your eyes open it would *seem* like three days, and you get what I mean, anyway. Then sometimes I spend the night in the Egyptian Room of the Metropolitan Museum of Art. Very nice. Also, occasionally, the Cloisters. You know the Cloisters?

GLAS   The what?

RANDALL   The Cloisters. Uptown.

GLAS   No.

RANDALL   That's the best place. Absolutely. It's a place they built like where them monks used to live a long time ago, you know? A monastery. All stone and cool and quiet with a lotta old wooden statues of saints and

Jesus Christ and people like that. That's the best place to sleep.

GLAS   They don't catch you?

RANDALL   No, I hide pretty good. They ain't never caught me yet . . . Yeah, I sure woulda liked to be one a them monks way back then. You believe in reincarnation?

GLAS   Reincarnation?

RANDALL   Yeah. You know, the perpetuation of the immortal soul by the device of it passin' into another body upon the death of this one? (GLAS *nods*) You believe in that?

GLAS   I don't know. I don't think so. No.

RANDALL   Ah. Well, *I* do. It can be a great comfort on occasion in this vale of tears, you be surprised. I was a courtier in the court of Lorenzo de Medici one a my other times. Fifteenth century . . . Yeah . . . (*Pause. For a moment, he is far away*) And anything I happen to need I got right here, of course. (*He opens his cape, which is lined, top to bottom, with zippered pockets*) You name it, I got it. No need for me to be borin' you with a complete and exhaustive inventory but like for an example I just earlier this evenin' acquired me this battery-operated toothbrush even. (*He displays this, switching it on and off*) Cain't hardly wait till tomorra mornin', see how it works. It either gonna give my teeth one hell of a brushin' or it gonna *electrocute* me, one or the other. (*He returns the gadget to the pocket in the cape*) So anyway, now I think I'm beginnin' to understand.

GLAS   Hm?

33

RANDALL   Your what we might call, your profound in-difference to the recent, uh—disposition of your fellow countryman, Mister Eichmann.

GLAS   What about it?

RANDALL   I mean, you not bein' a Jew and all. Here I been goin' on the false assumption that you was. Is. A Jewish man. That bein' the case, it been hard for me to reconcile the fact that you ain't been givin' a shit one way or the other about old Adolf here, swayin' gently to and fro, as they say, with a broken neck, ruptured larynx, deceased. But you *not* bein' a Jew, I now comprehend totally. Your indifference.

GLAS   You think only Jews care?

RANDALL   They do seem to be the ones most upset and distraught by the matter, yeah. I mean, they the ones who *hung* him. Seem to me somewhat bloodthirsty.

GLAS   What do *you* know about it?

RANDALL   What I read in the newspapers, baby.

GLAS   There's more to know than what you read in the newspapers, believe me.

RANDALL   Why.

GLAS   Because there is.

RANDALL   I mean why should I believe you?

GLAS   Because I know.

RANDALL   What do you know, daddy?

GLAS   I was there.

RANDALL   Where.

GLAS   Germany. In the camps.

RANDALL   Mm-hm. Thought you said you wasn't a Jew.

GLAS   What?

RANDALL   I don't understand what you was doin' in one a them concentration camp places, then. (*No response from* GLAS) I mean, you not bein' Jewish and all. I been under the impression that you hadda be Jewish to get inta one a them concentration places.

GLAS   You didn't have to be Jewish.

RANDALL   What else could you be to be allowed inta one a them camps?

GLAS   What do you mean, *allowed* in? What do you think, they were private hotels or something? (*Then, shouting*) What do you think!
      (*Pause*)

RANDALL   (*Quietly*) Don't be hollerin' at me, Mister Glas, sir. One thing do get me all upset and nervous is for someone to be hollerin' at me. I mean, we gettin' along just fine, so long as we be nice to each other and don't go raisin' our voices in the heat of anger, know what I mean?
      (GLAS *does not appear to be intimidated by the menace in* RANDALL'S *tone*)

GLAS   You're a real sensitive type, you are.

RANDALL   Oh, my, now! That what *she* used to be all the time sayin'. She was all the time sayin' that very thing. When I was just a little fella, you know? You're too sensitive for your own good, Randall. She said that quite a bit. She didn't understand, see what I mean? That I

35

am a dark and tortured soul, I mean. In need of compassion and understandin' just like them psychologists says. You gotta forgive me my trespasses and my sensitivities! . . . She don't say it no more, though, about me bein' too sensitive.

GLAS   Who.
   (*Pause*)

RANDALL   So what was you doin' in the concentration camp, then? If you wasn't a Jew?
   (*Pause*)

GLAS   I was a political prisoner, a Communist. (*He speaks this very quickly and turns away*)

RANDALL   Oh, man! That's *worse*! You was really a commonist?

GLAS   That's right.

RANDALL   You still? A commonist?

GLAS   No.

RANDALL   Uh, huh. So, what was it like, bein' in one a them concentration camps?

GLAS   You don't know?

RANDALL   How would *I* know? *I* ain't never been in one. Been in one or two places bearin' a close *resemblance* to concentration camps, but I am otherwise without firsthand knowledge of their true nature.

GLAS   Plenty of books around these days, tell you all about it.

RANDALL   Well, I do remember, durin' one a my brief periods in attendance at school, I do remember there bein' about a page and a half in the history book on the subject of concentration camps.

GLAS A page and a half.

RANDALL Yeah. And what with me havin' a IQ of a hundred and eighty-seven it crossed my mind at the time that there maybe might be a teeny bit more to that particular topic than a page and a half. I mean, readin' between the lines as I was.

GLAS Never read between the lines, sonny, there's nothing there.

RANDALL A point well taken, Mister Glas, sir. The truth of the matter is you'll find me to be unusually well-informed regardin' current and recent events in the world arena. But the thing is I ain't actually never met anybody who was *in* one a them concentration camps. So this here is a ideal opportunity for you to fill in one a them gaps in what might be referred to as my smörgåsbord education. (GLAS *smiles*) You got a real nice smile, Mister Glas, sir. You smiled more often you'd be winnin' friends and influencin' people all over the place.

GLAS I'm not interested in—

BOTH (*In unison*) Winning friends and influencing people.

RANDALL (*Nodding*) I know, I know. So what was it like, then?
    (*Pause.* GLAS, *when he speaks, is without emotion, his face a mask, his voice flat and dull*)

GLAS They broke my leg. In four places. Starting at the ankle and working their way up.

37

RANDALL (*Matter-of-fact, seemingly unmoved*)   Why'd they do that?

GLAS   Why?

RANDALL   Yeah. I mean, for what reason. Was it just it was a slow afternoon like and they had nothin' better to do, or what?

GLAS (*After a pause, as though he had not heard*)   And there was a time we found out that one of the prisoners had acquired some parts of a dead body and given them to the cook in return for certain favors. The cook kept the regular meat ration for himself and put the human flesh in the stew, which the prisoners ate.

RANDALL (*Quietly*)   Oh, man.

GLAS   When we found out, first we killed the cook. We stuffed his mouth with the meat, the human flesh, and pushed his head into the stew pot and held him under until he was dead. The next night we killed the other one, the prisoner. We picked him up, four of us, and threw him against the fence.
(*Pause*)

RANDALL   Yeah?

GLAS   Mm.

RANDALL   So?

GLAS   What?

RANDALL   What then. I mean, you threw him against the fence? That's all?

GLAS   It was wired, the fence. He was electrocuted.
(*Pause*)

RANDALL   *That's* cool.
(*Pause.* GLAS *descends the ladder with a box of cheap, stubby candles, places the box on the counter and proceeds to count the candles*)

GLAS   Of course, there are authenticated cases of cannibalism in the camps in which the people involved *knew* what they were eating. And continued without protest —to eat.

RANDALL   That a fact?

GLAS   They were hungry.

RANDALL   You gotta be pretty goddam hungry, though, huh?

GLAS   True.

RANDALL   I don't think I could ever get that hungry under no circumstances whatsoever.

GLAS   But you don't have to go back to those days and those places to find Nazis. It was Nazis put *that* there.

RANDALL   Which.

GLAS   That. That monstrosity, that noise box. What do you think it's doing here? One day two men come in and look around and ask me how would I like a juke box, give the place a little class? I say no, thanks just the same, I don't need no juke boxes today. They say, sure I do, they can tell just by looking at me that I need a juke box. I say no, still very polite. They say yes, only not so nice this time. I say no again, they say yes, I say definitely no. So the next night a brick through the window, glass flying all over the place, a cut on my head. So I have a juke box. And those men, they wear white ties with their black shirts, but around the eyes—just like the Nazis.

RANDALL You shoulda reported those gentlemen to your local law-enforcement authorities.

GLAS That's the first funny joke you made yet, sonny.

RANDALL I knew my sense of humor would make an impression on you sooner or later if I was just to keep at it.

GLAS (*Absently, a candle in his hand*) They light a candle.

RANDALL Say again?

GLAS A candle. Every year a bunch of Jewish people get together and light a fat candle for the six million Jews the Nazis killed. A candle. For six million people you light the sun, maybe. But a candle?

RANDALL Even a fat candle.

GLAS You even make a joke about that?
(*Pause. When* RANDALL *speaks now, the dialect is gone, there is no trace of the distorted speech rhythm, the frenetic delivery; and the level of the voice is lower and normal*)

RANDALL Perhaps a candle would do for the living, Mister Glas.
(*Pause.* GLAS *is clearly puzzled*)

GLAS What?

RANDALL What I mean to say is that if the dead require the sun, perhaps a mere candle would do for the living. Like you. Or me. Tell you what: the first chance I get, I'll light a candle for you. Place a small sign on it, perhaps: This candle for Mister Glas, exclusively. One of the living. (*He removes his glasses, calmly, and his hat, which he places carefully on the counter*) Don't be confused, Mister Glas, sir. It's just that sometimes . . . I run out of gas, so to speak.

GLAS Gas? What gas? Listen—

RANDALL Well, I mean, energy. What I mean to say is that it requires a great deal of energy to be what one isn't. For any extended length of time. You'd be surprised how much energy is required—which cannot be sustained indefinitely. Also, it always bores me finally.

GLAS You talk different.

RANDALL True, true. Precisely.

GLAS What are you, some kind of an actor or something?

RANDALL Not exactly, no.

GLAS What do you mean, not exactly? What kind of funny business—

RANDALL I mean only to the extent that we all are. Do you know what I mean?
    (*Pause*)

GLAS I don't know and I don't care. There's the door, sonny. You go out just the way you come in and we won't have any trouble around here, okay?

RANDALL (*In dialect again*) You gettin' me all wrong, daddy. Ain't gonna be no trouble, no-how.
(*Pause*)

GLAS I think maybe I call the cops.
(*He turns toward the telephone on the wall, but before he can take a second step,* RANDALL *is there; he rips the receiver from the box, returns to* GLAS *and hands it to him, the cord dangling*)

RANDALL Say hello for me. (GLAS *stares*) You can go and get them if you like, of course. The police. I won't stop you. (*He backs away from* GLAS *with a permissive gesture toward the door.* GLAS, *after considering a moment, takes a tentative step toward the door, watching* RANDALL *cautiously.* RANDALL *speaks again in the dialect*) 'Course they ain't no tellin' how far *away* they be. And there ain't no way of tellin' what this place look like by the time you get back. And they ain't *absolutely* no way of tellin' where *I* be by that time.
(*Silence.* GLAS *moves finally, not looking at* RAN-DALL, *apparently absorbed in thought.* RANDALL *watches closely, smiling, waiting for* GLAS *to make the next move and knowing what it will be.* GLAS *makes it: a lunge behind the counter, groping. He comes up in a rage*)

GLAS Where is it!

RANDALL What's that.

GLAS (*Quietly, knowing already*) The gun, goddam it.

RANDALL Oh, that. That's in my pocket, yes.

GLAS Stupid!

RANDALL Me?

GLAS (*After a pause, grinning humorlessly*) No, not you.

RANDALL I don't know why you're getting so upset, Mister Glas, I truly don't.

GLAS What do you want?

RANDALL Nothing.

GLAS Tell me what you want, you take it and you leave, hah?

RANDALL What makes you think I want something? Have I asked you for anything?

GLAS Why don't you just go away and leave me alone. I don't want any trouble.
    (RANDALL *is at the street door, looking into the street*)

RANDALL If *I* were you I'd write a letter to the mayor or something about that. No street lights: very bad for business, no street lights. Who wants to walk down a dark street, any more? (*He adds, in the dialect*) 'Ceptin maybe chaps like me. I mean, there is a certain fear and tension amongst the populace, you know what I mean? And a reluctance to venture down dark streets. (*Then again, naturally, quietly*) A reluctance to venture down dark streets.
    (*He begins to hum again, the same tune*)

GLAS What's the idea with you, anyway?

RANDALL   What idea is that, Mister Glas, sir?

GLAS   The funny talk and the phony stories. What's the idea with all that?

RANDALL (*Still at the door, his back to* GLAS)   You do me wrong, Mister Glas, sir: I speak only the truth.

GLAS   All that about being a genius, that's the truth, hah? (RANDALL *nods, indifferently*) You don't look like a genius to me.

RANDALL   What does a genius look like, Mister Glas?
          (*Pause*)

GLAS   And about not having any place to live, that's the truth, hah? (*No response from* RANDALL) Everyone lives someplace. (*No response*) I suppose you were born with a hole in your heart too.

RANDALL   During a partial eclipse of the sun.

GLAS   Naturally.

RANDALL   True, all true. Truly. Actually it's the only thing in my life for which I have an explanation, the hole in my heart, making it unique and something to be clung to at all costs. Randall, you see, was conceived of a union between his mother and one of the numberless men she never saw again, his mother being a prostitute by profession. Conceived of lust and the natural hungers of the flesh, but without love. It was that absence of love that left the hole in Randall's heart, no mistake. Of course, the realization of that fact was not to come to Randall until somewhat later on in his life,' but picture, if you will, Randall, at the age of approximately six months when his momma begun to notice a rather alarming fact regarding his overall physical condition, the fact bein' that little Randall hadn't grown an inch, not a little bitty inch since the day of his birth. So she took him off down to the hospital, his momma did, and what do you think they discovered? What do you think? Why they discovered that little Randall's heart hadn't healed up all the way, like it was supposed to, like everyone else's, while he was still in his momma's womb. A comparatively rare occurrence, indeed. So they executed with great skill and care a delicate operation and sewed up that nasty hole in Randall's wee heart. From then on, of course, it was in and out of hospitals for the child Randall and he couldn't play roughlike with the other children and he had to take things easy in general and his momma said to everyone that little Randall had been born with a hole in his heart, can you imagine such a thing, a hole in his heart, she didn't have troubles enough in this misery of a life. A colloquial expression, that, a hole in the heart, but true. True. She used it often. It got so that Randall began to think if he heard that expression one more time he be about ready to cut somebody's throat, it being a toss-up whether it would be his own or his momma's. He was saved from the perpetration of that rash act, however, by the fact that at about that time his momma was apprehended for offerin' her charms to a officer of the law. Funny thing is he didn't arrest her until after he'd *accepted* her offer. Know what I mean? Reason I know is, I was in the closet at the time, watchin', unbeknownst to momma and her gentleman visitor who proved subsequently to be a officer of the law. I was seven years old at the time, and fond of playin' in momma's closet. Poor momma. That old cop gettin' up offa her and pullin' up his pants and flashin' his shiny old badge, was she surprised. Mad too, of course, but mostly surprised, I remember that very clear. That was her third arrest for lewd and lascivious behavior and naturally they didn't believe her no-how about the hanky-panky that went on with her and the arrestin' officer *prior* to the arrest, and nobody thought to ask *me* were it true or not, which I woulda said it was since I seen it with my very own eyes, and she got detained for ninety days in the Women's House of Detention. It was durin' that time of her detention that somebody or other took high offense at the fact of me striking one of my playmates lightly on the face without first taking the precaution of removing the beer can opener from my hand, an oversight which made for quite a little bit of a mess so far as the little chap's face was concerned, you might be able to imagine. So, my momma bein' elsewhere occupied and me bein' otherwise kinless, they up and put me in a kinda *home*. That's where they first discovered about me bein' so smart and all 'cause at the time I was carryin' in my pocket a book of poems which I had acquired free of charge under somewhat surreptitious circumstances and which had been authored by someone whose name I couldn't pronounce and they said what was I doin' with that book, a book like that, and I said readin' it. And one thing led to another, you know how those things are, and they discovered that I was extraordinarily smart. Then after a while, they let me go back to my momma who was free and swingin'

again. Now you have a kinda montage effect showin'
momma plyin' her trade and Randall gettin' the picture
very gradual but very clear and this goes on for several
years, Randall listenin' to the men clompin' up the
stairs with his momma and down again alone, leavin'
momma in the bedroom with the sound of running
water. About that time was when she stopped usin' that
expression. You know: about the hole in Randall's heart?
She stopped usin' it and Randall started. Had a nice
ring to it, that expression, and it explained a lotta things
just right. I mean, every time he did something called
wrong, well of course, naturally: he had a hole in his
heart, that's why. What could be simpler, I submit to
you? Like for instance, the pigeons. Randall had a flock
of pigeons, fourteen pigeons in a coop on the roof. And
one day very sudden, very sudden, they began to die,
those pigeons. They began to die of a disease Randall
didn't know anything about. Every morning when he
went up to the coop, there would be another pigeon,
lying stiff and dead. Which was a very sad thing for
Randall, because he loved those pigeons, he truly did.
Loved them. But then a peculiar and interesting change
came over Randall in his feelings toward his pigeons.
He began to hate them instead. I mean, after he got
through hating whatever it was that was killing his beautiful birds, he began to hate the birds themselves, he
began to hate them for just up and dying on him, in that
tantalizing way they had, one by one, dyin' one by one.
So the birds that were left, he killed them. There were
six of them left and one day he strangled them, one by
one, with a piece of string. And a little boy on the roof
next door stood there watchin', and sayin', Why are

47

you doin' that, Randall, why are you doin' that thing like that? And Randall just standin' there with his birds scattered around dead at his feet, sayin' to himself, Because I got a hole in my heart, why do you think? Randall was twelve years old at that time. Then the time some years later and Randall is in the process of fleein' the scene of a crime, as they say, when a thirty-eight caliber bullet fired from the gun bein' held steadily in the hand of one of New York's Finest, marksmen all, when that bullet entered his back just under the left shoulder blade and lodged against the back side of a rib, the force of the blow propelling Randall some ten feet or so right into the gutter on his face. And there Randall lay with his mouth in a little river of rain water, shot through the heart. Oh, you know what the doctors said, naturally they said that bullet had struck him just an inch *below* the heart, but he knew better, Randall did. He knew goddamned well that little old bullet had passed right through the hole in his heart and out the other side. He did not share this knowledge with the constituted authorities, however, feelin' rightly that they would be disinclined to accept his explanation. Follows two years of restitution for Randall in a woodsy little correctional farm for youthful offenders in the upper reaches of New York State. And wouldn't you know that on attainin' his freedom, who should be standin' there to greet him at the train station but his dear little momma? His momma who wrote him three letters in two years and never did manage to make him a visit in the flesh. But there she is, standin' in a silky green dress and a white hat, sayin', Welcome home, Randall, you lookin' just fine. And Randall just look at her right in

the eye for about a minute or two and says real quiet,
Go away, Mama. Which disturbs her no end, for some
reason or other, and sets her to screaming on a gradu-
ated scale of pitch and intensity, following Randall
across the marble vastness of the Grand Central Station
and all the folks lookin' on and listenin' to the flashy,
colored lady makin' all that racket, they're so uninhibited
and spontaneous, those people. Her screamin' I'm your
momma, Randall, I'm your momma no matter what,
and various and assorted other demands of endearment.
And the last thing Randall hears before he hit the top
of the stairs, leavin' his mother puffin' at the bottom,
the last thing he hears was her screamin', You got no
love in you, Randall, you're all mean and black inside
and you got no love in you! Which was all too true,
of course. Because, that piece which had never grown
into Randall's heart? . . . That was the place where love
is. Of course. (*Pause*) Never make a long story short,
that's my motto. (*Pause*) "Our fathers, viler than our
grandfathers, begot us who are even viler, and we shall
bring forth a progeny more degenerate still." . . . You
know who said that? (*He waits for an answer, then
turns to look at* GLAS *who stares*) Horace said that. Ro-
man poet. Born sixty-five B.C., died eight B.C. Horace
being a pseudonym, his true name being Quintus Ho-
ratius Flaccus. I quoted that to a probation officer once
and told him Horace said that and he said, Horace
who? But then, I can't be altogether too harsh on him,
he wasn't blessed with an IQ of one hundred and eighty-
seven and the necessity to know the truth. (*Pause*) Is
your silence a profound one, Mister Glas? (GLAS *only
gazes.* RANDALL *speaks again in the dialect*) Silence also

49

speaks, daddy. (*Sings quietly*) I went to the rock to hide my face, the rock cried out, no hiding place . . .

(*Behind* RANDALL *the door bursts open; he wheels, wielding the umbrella, prepared to strike. Standing in the doorway is a girl of nineteen, singularly plain-looking, with orange hair that falls to her shoulders; and eyeglasses. She is wearing a blue denim skirt and a black cotton pullover and sandals. Her name is* ROSIE)

ROSIE (*With mingled rage and frustration, imploringly, near to tears*)   Where the hell is the goddamn Brooklyn Bridge?

(*She releases her hold on the knob of the door, takes a single step into the room, and faints.* RANDALL *and* GLAS *are as still as she while the curtain falls on Act One*)

Act Two

Pas de Trois

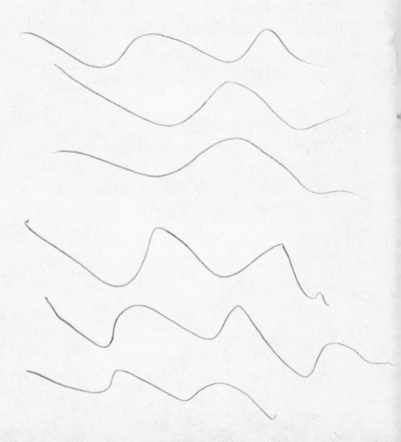

ACT TWO

Scene One

A moment has passed; all are as before. Then GLAS *moves, stooping to the girl.*

GLAS Miss? . . . Miss!
    (*Distraught, he slaps her face lightly, tentatively.* RANDALL *puts on his sunglasses and hat, slowly.* GLAS *looks about for a moment, disorganized. Then he gets to his feet and exits quickly into the rear of the store, ignoring* RANDALL. RANDALL's *eye falls upon the ladder and he moves leisurely to it. He looks up, then climbs to the very top and sits, his chin in his hands, surveying the scene.* GLAS *re-enters carrying a large bottle; he notes* RANDALL's *absence and looks around quickly, but not up, and assumes him to be gone. He stoops to the girl, removes the cap from the bottle, lifts her head and holds the bottle under her nose, wafting it. She comes awake choking and coughing*)

ROSIE Jesus! (*She grasps the bottle, looking at the label, pushing it away*) Ammonia! Jesus!

GLAS Are you all right?

ROSIE (*Sitting up now, groggy*) I fainted.

GLAS Yes. Are you all right?

ROSIE I know it sounds corny as hell but where am I?

GLAS My name is Glas. This is my place, my store.

ROSIE   I *am* in Brooklyn, though, right?

GLAS   Oh, yes.

ROSIE   I got lost. Goddamned BMT.

GLAS   You're looking for the Brooklyn Bridge?

ROSIE   Yeah. At this point I'm strongly considering jumping off it.

GLAS   I beg your pardon?

ROSIE   I think I can get up now.
  (GLAS *assists her to her feet*)

GLAS   Maybe you better sit here for a little bit, hah?
  (*He guides her to a stool at the counter. She sits, picks up the newspaper, glances at the headline*)

ROSIE   Oh, they hung the bastard, huh? Good.
  (*She drops the paper*)

GLAS   I should call a doctor for you maybe, hah?

ROSIE   No, no, that won't be necessary. But, listen, I'll tell you something that would help out a lot.

GLAS   Anything at all.

ROSIE   Is there a bathroom around?

GLAS   You're going to be sick?

ROSIE   Well, no. It's just I've been walking all over Brooklyn for hours and I have to go to the bathroom pretty bad.

GLAS   (*Disconcerted*)   Oh, I see. Oh . . . Well, yes, I got a bathroom, sure. Straight back through there, the second door on the lefthand side of the hallway.

ROSIE   Thank you very much.

> (*She goes to the door and exits.* GLAS *watches after her for a moment, then his attention is caught by* RANDALL's *empty soda bottle on the counter. He picks it up, looks at the door to the street. Pause.* RANDALL *blows his nose.* GLAS *whirls and discovers* RANDALL *atop the ladder*)

GLAS   (*After a pause*)   I thought you were gone. (*No response from* RANDALL) I don't know what to do about you.

RANDALL   (*In the dialect*)   *Do* about me? Ain't nothin' you gotta *do* about me, daddy.

GLAS   If you're going to rob me why don't you do it now and get it over with, and leave me alone. Take what you want and leave. I would appreciate it if you would return the pistol, it cost me thirty-three dollars, even second hand, which is a lot of money for me. I wouldn't shoot you or try to stop you or anything.

RANDALL   (*Naturally*)   Suppose I were to tell you that I have no intention whatsoever of robbing you, Mister Glas, sir?

GLAS   You're telling me that?

RANDALL   (*In the dialect*)   No, I ain't *tellin'* you, I said *suppose* I was to tell you that. Would you believe me to be tellin' the absolute truth?

GLAS   I don't know.

RANDALL   You don't know?
> (*Pause*)

GLAS   Okay, I would believe you if you told me that.

RANDALL (*Naturally*) Okay, then I'm telling you.

GLAS What do you want here, then?

RANDALL (*Dialect*) You pretty hipped on that there subject, ain't you.

GLAS What?

RANDALL I say your mind occupied to a considerable extent with that subject, ain't it.

GLAS What subject?

RANDALL What I want. You all the time sayin' you don't understand what I want and I'm all the time tellin' you I don't want *nothin'*. What is it make you think I gotta be *wantin'* somethin'? I asked you for anything yet? *Nothin'*. So what so difficult to understand about that? I merely come trippin' merrily into here, real casual-like, to pass the time of the evenin' and right away you figurin' me to cut you up and *rob* you, or somethin'! You been watchin' too much of the TV, that the problem with you, I think, and lettin' your imagination run *riot*, as they say.

GLAS I don't have a TV.

RANDALL Whooee, you a difficult man, indeed.

GLAS In the first place, you didn't come in here casual, you came in here running. I saw you.

RANDALL We already decided that to be a matter of opinion, I been thinkin'—the truth not always bein' found in the eye of the beholder. What about in the second place?

GLAS In the second place, someone who destroys my property and steals my pistol for which I had to apply to the

Police Department for a special permit, otherwise it's against the law— Not to mention the fact of all this funny talk when you can speak as good as me. That's in the third place. Why do you talk like that if you can talk properly?

RANDALL A matter of self-induced schizophrenia, purely. You lookin' at the Doctor Jekyll and Mister Hyde of the Negro race, daddy.

GLAS You mock yourself.

RANDALL (*Naturally*) Perhaps not myself.

GLAS What about my telephone?

RANDALL Yes, well . . .

GLAS Who's going to pay for that, hah?

RANDALL (*Dialect*) Oh, man! no need for you to be worryin' yourself about that. Telephone Company take care of that easy. Neighborhood like this, they figure they comin' out ahead if the *rest* of it still attached to the wall. So whatta you figure *she* wants, then? . . . The little chick with the orange hair currently occupyin' your bathroom.

GLAS How do I know what she wants? The Brooklyn Bridge, she says.

RANDALL Which sound to me suspicious in the *extreme*. Don't it hit you somewhat suspicious? (*Before* GLAS *can reply, the glow from a flashing red light is thrown into the store from the street and with it a very brief groan of a siren: a police car has parked at the curb and announced its presence.* RANDALL *scrambles down the ladder, then stands very still*) I do believe that be the cops.

57

(GLAS *moves; so does* RANDALL, *and with an almost imperceptible movement of the umbrella.* GLAS *stops and regards* RANDALL *and the umbrella*)

GLAS   They won't come in if I go out. (*Silence*) They come every night—for a bottle of soda and an ice-cream pop. They don't come in, I take it out to them. Curb service, hah? (RANDALL *is not amused*) They won't come in if I go out. (*A brief pause before* RANDALL *steps cautiously, still uncertain, out of* GLAS's *path.* GLAS *goes to the door, opens it and calls out*) I'll be right with you, hah?

(*He moves to the rear of the counter, gets two bottles of soda, opens them, and two ice-cream pops; he returns to the door and exits into the street. He is gone for several moments during which* RANDALL *stands motionless, tensed and waiting, his eyes on the door.* GLAS *reappears in the doorway and returns* RANDALL's *gaze. The police car is heard pulling away.* GLAS *closes the door*)

RANDALL (*Naturally*)   You're a very confusing man, Mister Glas.

GLAS   It's a confusing life, sonny. (RANDALL *takes the revolver from within the cape and places it on the counter. Pause*) The bullets? You don't want to take the bullets out?

(RANDALL *regards the gun a moment before turning and slowly re-ascending the ladder.* GLAS *takes the revolver and replaces it on its hook behind the counter.* ROSIE *enters, freshened*)

ROSIE   Well, that's a vast improvement.

GLAS   How do you feel?

ROSIE Well, the truth is, all that's the matter with me is I haven't eaten anything in about twenty-four hours. You don't happen to have any food here, do you? Like a sandwich or something?
(*She sits on a stool*)

GLAS Candy and ice cream. Soda. Coffee. Pastry—but it's stale.

ROSIE Is there anyplace around here I could get something to eat?

GLAS Not this time of night. You really haven't eaten anything in all that time?

ROSIE No. What time is it, anyway?

RANDALL 'Cordin' to my twenny-one jewel, Swiss movement chronometer watch it now seventeen and a half minutes past eleven o'clock in the evenin' of June the first, nineteen hundred and sixty-two.
(ROSIE, *of course, is startled*)

ROSIE Who's he?

RANDALL Randall.

GLAS *This* week. (*The private joke is acknowledged between* RANDALL *and* GLAS, *leaving* ROSIE *somewhat confused, but she lets it pass*) Don't pay any attention to him.

ROSIE It's a little hard not to pay any attention to a guy with an umbrella and sunglasses sitting on top of a ladder in a candy store, but I'll try if you think it's the best thing. (*She looks up at* RANDALL, *smiles*) Randall, was it? (RANDALL *nods*) Hello, Randall.

RANDALL Hidi, little chick!

ROSIE Rosie.

RANDALL Rosie. Welcome back to the realm of the conscious, Rosie.

ROSIE Thank you very much.

GLAS All right, *stop* that talk will you, goddamnit. (*To* ROSIE) He doesn't really talk that way.

ROSIE I beg your pardon?

GLAS He doesn't really talk that way. Come down off the goddamn ladder now!
    (*Pause.* GLAS *is glaring at* RANDALL. RANDALL *is wiping the lenses of his glasses with a handkerchief —without removing them from his eyes, however.* ROSIE *looks from one to the other, wants no part of either of them, and steps down from the stool*)

ROSIE Well, I guess I'll be going, then, okay?

GLAS No, wait. I think you should rest maybe for—

ROSIE Look, I don't know what kind of a nuthouse I fell into here, but I'm just not really in the mood for it tonight. Any other night, okay, it might prove to be interesting, but tonight, no, definitely no. (*She takes two steps and is forced to support herself against the counter*) Oh, boy.

GLAS (*Moving quickly to her aid*) You're not well, miss. I should call a doctor, I think.

ROSIE (*Picking up the receiver*) Call a doctor?

GLAS Goddamnit! (*Turns to* RANDALL) You see now?

ROSIE No, it's all right, I was only kidding. I'll be okay in no time at all. What time did you say it was? Just the hour, I *know* what year it is.

RANDALL 'Leven-thirty.

ROSIE Well, it's too late now even if I could find it. (*She sighs and sits on the stool*)

RANDALL The Brooklyn Bridge?
(*She takes a slip of paper from her purse, hands it to* GLAS)

ROSIE You know where that is, that address?

GLAS Never heard of that street.

RANDALL Lemme see there. (*He descends the ladder, takes the paper, looks at it a moment, thinks*) Oh, yeah, yeah. That right near by to the—

ROSIE and RANDALL (*Unison*) *Brooklyn Bridge.*

RANDALL You a *long* way from the Brooklyn Bridge, little chick, a *long* way.

ROSIE I already figured that out, thanks.

RANDALL Ain't surprised you couldn't find that there place, though, it one a them funny streets, maybe two, three blocks long, you know? Also a pretty wild neighborhood for a little chick like yourself to be lookin' for in the middle of a night. A unsavory locale, you might say.

ROSIE Yeah, well, it's too late now, anyway. I was supposed to be there three hours ago. I should have known better than to have ever set my foot in Brooklyn. Brooklyn baffles me totally.

GLAS   Where are you from, miss?

ROSIE   A million miles away: the Bronx. Riverdale, actually. You know Riverdale?

GLAS   No.

ROSIE   Don't bother. If I don't get something to eat pretty soon I'm going to faint dead away on your floor again. (*Searching in her purse for change*) I'll have a couple of candy bars, at least, and maybe a bottle of soda.

RANDALL   I recommend the lemon.

GLAS   No. I'll fix you something decent to eat. Come on.

ROSIE   Where?

GLAS   In back.

ROSIE   (*Instantly suspicious, of course*) What's in back?

GLAS   My house. My kitchen.

ROSIE   Oh. Well, listen, you don't have to go to all that—

GLAS   You haven't eaten in twenty-four hours?

ROSIE   Something like that, but—

GLAS   You take a sandwich and a glass of milk.

ROSIE   Well, if it's not too much trouble . . .

GLAS   No trouble. Then you go back to Riverside and get a good night's sleep.

ROSIE   Yeah. River*dale.*

GLAS   Riverdale. (*He waits*) So?

ROSIE   Okay. Thanks very much. (*She steps down from the stool and starts toward the door where* GLAS *waits.*

She stops when she reaches him) Who's going to watch the store?

RANDALL What's to steal?

(GLAS *turns through the doorway, followed by* ROSIE, *who looks over her shoulder at* RANDALL *as she exits.* RANDALL *stands motionless, watching after them, uninvited.* GLAS *appears at the kitchen door, snaps on the light and steps into the room: it is an ordinary, clean, well-kept place. There is a covered canary cage on a stand; and, on the refrigerator, a bowl with several goldfish.* ROSIE *follows* GLAS *into the room. Then* GLAS *stops and is thoughtful for a moment*)

GLAS Wait a minute. (*He exits again and reappears at the store doorway.* RANDALL *has not moved*) All right, come on. (*He turns again, this time followed by* RANDALL, *whose face is expressionless.* GLAS *enters the kitchen.* RANDALL *stops at the kitchen doorway, lounging, not entering the room.* GLAS *speaks to* ROSIE) Sit.

(*She does and* GLAS *makes preparations to serve her food*)

ROSIE Where'd you get that outfit, Randall? Barney's Boy's Town?

RANDALL (*Smiles*) You very sharp, you know it, little chick?

ROSIE I know. Like my stepfather says, sharp as a tack and just as flat-headed. He's full of terribly clever remarks like that.

RANDALL I didn't say nothin' about the shape of your head, I only said you was very sharp, which is true.

63

ROSIE   Yeah, well, for once he was right.

RANDALL   Hm?

ROSIE   My stepfather.

RANDALL   Ah.
(GLAS *places bread, cheese, butter and milk before her on the table*)

ROSIE   I certainly appreciate this.

GLAS   What's the idea going such a long time without eating, hah?

ROSIE   Well, the doctor told me I wasn't supposed to eat anything for eight hours at least, so, true to my fashion, I overdid it—like everything else.

GLAS   What doctor?

ROSIE   The doctor I had the appointment with tonight who lives on the street nobody ever heard of.

GLAS   A doctor tells you not to eat? What kind of a doctor is that?

ROSIE   Well, he's an abortionist, as a matter of fact. He probably engages in a number of other unsavory medical practices but my particular business with him is in his capacity as an abortionist.
(*Silence*)

GLAS   What do you want with a doctor like that?

ROSIE (*Obviously*)   I'm pregnant.
(*Pause*)

GLAS   Oh?

ROSIE (*Nodding, with a mouthful of sandwich*)   Mm.

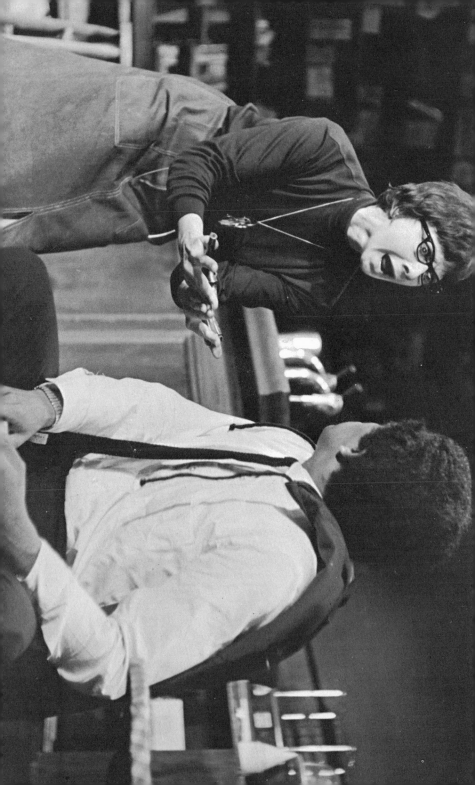

RANDALL It would appear, then, that you stubbed your toe, so to speak, while makin' your way along life's highway?

ROSIE Very well put.

GLAS You're, uh . . . you're going to a doctor?

ROSIE It's either that or get myself a knitting needle and have a go at it myself, which I'm not about to do.

GLAS But, what I mean . . . you don't want the child?

ROSIE *Hell,* no.

RANDALL You a pretty outspoken type, ain't you, little chick?

ROSIE Am I shocking you? (*Turns to* GLAS *without waiting for an answer*) It happens every day, you know. And I have no patience with all the whispered-behind-the-hand hypocrisy about the facts of life, however sordid they may sometimes be. Right out in the open, that's my motto. *Right out in the open.* You wouldn't happen to have some peanut butter, would you? That I could put on this?

GLAS Peanut butter? Sure, I think maybe I got some peanut butter.

RANDALL You gonna put peanut butter on *cheese?*

ROSIE Ridiculous, isn't it? All week I've had this stupid *craving* for peanut butter and American cheese sandwiches. It's perfectly ridiculous. You know: cravings during pregnancy? It really burns me every time a cliché turns out to be true after all.

(GLAS *hands her the peanut butter, which she proceeds to spread on the cheese sandwich*)

GLAS So you're not married then, hah?

ROSIE No.

GLAS What about the man who, uh . . . ?

ROSIE Knocked me up? No. You married, Mister Glas?

GLAS Me?

ROSIE Yeah.
(*Pause*)

GLAS I was. She's dead. Why?

ROSIE Just curious. What camp were you in, Mister Glas?

GLAS Mm?

ROSIE In Germany. What concentration camp were you in?

GLAS How do you know I was in a camp?

ROSIE The tattoo.
(GLAS *glances briefly at the number tattooed on the inside of his left forearm*)

RANDALL Oh, man, is that what that is? Here I been thinkin' maybe it been his Social Security number, or somethin'.

ROSIE Oh, that's funny, that's really funny. You're a regular three-act comedy, aren't you.

GLAS He isn't as stupid as he would like you to think. (*To* RANDALL) Why don't you stop now with the funny talk. (*To* ROSIE) He doesn't really talk like that.
(ROSIE *looks at* RANDALL, *then at* GLAS, *then again at* RANDALL. *She is apparently disinclined to pursue the matter and resumes eating*)

ROSIE   Well, anyway, congratulations.

GLAS   Hm?

ROSIE   On your survival.

RANDALL   They busted his leg in four places, though.

ROSIE   A lot of my grandfather's family were in the camps. But they didn't make it out. Their name was Kasner. Ever run across them? (GLAS *shakes his head*) You're not Jewish, are you.

GLAS   No.

ROSIE   Political then, huh?

RANDALL   He a commonist, Mister Glas is.

ROSIE   Are you?

GLAS   I was at the time.

RANDALL   Once a commonist, always a commonist.

ROSIE   (*Drily*) *That*'s an interesting political philosophy.

RANDALL   Ain't no political philosophy, little chick. That's an *opinion*. You ought never to be confusin' opinions with political philosophies.

ROSIE   Score one for you, Randall. (*To* GLAS) You're right: he's not so dumb.

RANDALL   I knew I be winnin' you over sooner or later with my charm and brilliance of expression, yes indeed.

ROSIE   (*To* GLAS) I'm doing a thesis on the camps.

GLAS   Hm?

ROSIE   A thesis. *You* know, a college term paper, Modern History.

67

GLAS Ah.

ROSIE Maybe you'd like to contribute.

GLAS Contribute?

ROSIE Well, I've been interviewing some survivors, you know? Getting some fantastic stories, actually. I mean, it's one thing to read about the kinds of things that went on in the camps, you know, but to hear it, to watch someone's lips speaking the words, to see the eyes. The worst thing I've heard was about the cannibalism. Only one man that I've interviewed so far, but even one. He said it seemed more terrible in retrospect than it did at the time. I can see how that might be true. An interesting thing about that particular man, though: he doesn't eat pork. It occurred to me, so I asked him. You know what I mean? He ate human flesh once, but he won't eat pork, because it's against his religion, of course.

RANDALL He ain't hungry enough.

ROSIE Yeah, I suppose. But anyway, maybe you could answer a few questions about your experience. I've been getting mostly Jews, very few political prisoners.

GLAS No, no questions.

ROSIE Oh ... May I ask why?

GLAS I got no answers.

ROSIE Oh. Well, I understand.
(GLAS *gazes at her*)

RANDALL "Please do not understand me too quickly." (*To* ROSIE) You know who said that? André Gide said that. (ROSIE *is mildly impressed at this*) Where you in attendance at college, little chick?

ROSIE   NYU. Where else? (*Still intrigued at* RANDALL's *knowledge of Gide, she turns to* GLAS) He wanted to send me to Vassar, old stepdaddy, but I wasn't having any of that, thank you very much. All those trees, all that ivy, it would've driven me right out of my skull. I'm strictly a city girl. New York, New York, where the natives talk like machine guns, that's for me.

GLAS   Listen, uh—Rosie. About this other business.

ROSIE   What other business?

GLAS   About you. I mean, this—doctor, the . . .

ROSIE   The abortion, you mean.

GLAS   Yes.

ROSIE   You don't like the word.

GLAS   It's an ugly word.

ROSIE   There are no ugly words, Mister Glas. It's a perfectly good word. *Abortion.* See? The roof didn't fall in. What about it?

GLAS   It's not a good thing.

ROSIE   Good, bad. It's necessary. You know?

GLAS   Why.

ROSIE   Why! Well, that's perfectly obvious, isn't it? I'm not married, for one thing.

GLAS   You couldn't get married?

ROSIE   Ho, boy! Who'd marry *me?*

RANDALL   I'd marry you, little chick.

ROSIE   Thanks anyway, we both have enough problems.

GLAS   What do you mean, who would marry you? Why not?

ROSIE   Look, Mister Glas, there are a lot of things I don't have. Among the things I don't have are illusions. I have no illusions about myself. Or anything else for that matter. You know what I mean?

GLAS   No.

ROSIE   Take a good look at me, Mister Glas. Homely is homely, no matter how you slice it. I'm nobody's dream-girl.

RANDALL   Everybody is *somebody's* dream-girl, little chick.

ROSIE   Look, uh—Randall: be anything you like but don't be naïve, okay? Naïveté is a bore. You know how in the movies this girl with glasses takes them off and suddenly everybody in the room falls down at the sheer beauty of her?

RANDALL   I seen that picture, yeah.

ROSIE   Look.
        (*She removes her eyeglasses. Pause*)

RANDALL   I see what you mean, yeah.
        (*She replaces the eyeglasses*)

GLAS   What about the young man?

ROSIE   Which.

GLAS   You know: the one . . .

ROSIE   Oh, the responsible party, you mean.

GLAS   Yes.

ROSIE   As a way out, my way is better. *Believe* me.

GLAS You couldn't be married to him?

ROSIE No.

GLAS He won't, hah?

ROSIE What, marry me? (GLAS *nods*) I don't know, I haven't asked him.

RANDALL 'Cordin' to my understandin' of the usual procedure, it supposed to be the other way around.

ROSIE I don't think either of you have quite grasped the picture here. In the first place, the guy doesn't even know about it, that I'm pregnant. In the second place, I haven't *seen* him since the afternoon of our Grand Passion. In the third place, I wouldn't tell him I was pregnant if I *did* see him. In the fifth place—

RANDALL Fourth place.

ROSIE Fourth place, thank you. In the fourth place, I have no intention of getting married. Even if he were to make the offer, which I doubt. And in the *fifth* place —(*She nods to* RANDALL, *who nods in return*) I *certainly* have no intention of having a kid, since I have other plans, career-wise.

GLAS Ah.

ROSIE I'm going to be a writer, you see, and—

RANDALL That a fact?

ROSIE Mm. And obviously a child at this time could not possibly be on the agenda.

RANDALL What kinda books you gonna write, little chick?

ROSIE Good ones.

71

RANDALL Yeah, but—

ROSIE Novels.

RANDALL Oh, man. You ain't gonna be one a them lady writers write them strange-type books, are ya?

ROSIE What strange-type books?

RANDALL Well, I mean, like this one book I read once by a lady writer all about this here little girl in Alabama or someplace southern like that, she about ten years old with her hair cut very short which she cut off with her father's straight-razor and she wears overhalls all the time and no shoes? And like she has this cousin who is an alcoholic—or maybe he was a homosexual—anyway, he has *some* kinda problem. And he has this girl friend who is intimated subtly in the book to be his sister, I wasn't quite sure about that, but there's this scene where they're in a old shack way the hell out in the woods and he's burnin' the soles of her feet while she's doin' somethin', you know, sexual to him—it wasn't quite clear to me what, but it was definitely unauthorized behavior. Then this little girl who is the main person in the story, she's supposed to be in love with this here midget who don't have no legs, you know, wheels himself around in a little red wagon? But she's supposed to love this midget without the legs quite a bit, no mistake. Only problem was, near as I could figure out, the midget, he's queer for his *cat* . . . you know?

  (*A short pause*)

ROSIE (*Deadpan*) Was the cat a male or a female?
  (*A short pause*)

RANDALL (*Deadpan*) That were never precisely specified.

72

(ROSIE *smiles, finally, and is about to speak when* GLAS *interrupts*)

GLAS   Listen, Rosie, I'm just thinking . . . how about you tell this young man about . . . your condition, hah?

ROSIE   Mister Glas, I appreciate your interest and concern, but there's no point in pursuing these hypothetical conjectures, there really isn't. I know what I'm doing.

GLAS   Listen, Rosie, you got to think, in the long run—

ROSIE   Oh, the *long* run, the *long* run! That's all I ever hear! The long run this, the long run that! What about the *short* run! I mean, what do you know about it? I'm the one with this, this *thing* floating blissfully around in my womb, feeding off me, draining me of all the juices of my life, ruining all my plans! Don't talk to me about *long* runs! (*An abrupt silence; all are still*) I'm sorry.

GLAS   (*Patting her hand*)   That's all right . . . It's all right. (GLAS *rises to serve the coffee.* ROSIE *removes her hair, which proves to be a wig.* RANDALL *is silent, but fascinated.* GLAS, *his back to the girl, does not immediately see. She takes a comb from her purse and proceeds to comb the wig.* GLAS *turns to the table with the coffee cups and is brought up short.* ROSIE, *becoming aware of his still figure, looks up from the wig, then smiles, sadly*)

ROSIE   One of my attempts at glamour. I like to think it helps, but I guess not. One has to remember the line about silk purses out of sow's ears.

RANDALL   You know who said that?

ROSIE   Yes, Randall, I know who said that. (*To* GLAS) Face it, I'm a sow's ear of the first water.

GLAS (*Annoyed*) What is all this talk about how you look? What's the matter with how you look?

ROSIE (*Continuing to comb the wig*) Tell me I'm beautiful, Mister Glas, I dare you.

GLAS Beautiful! What does that mean, beaut—

RANDALL You know what they say about beauty, little chick.

ROSIE (*Without looking at him*) You tell me beauty is only skin deep, Randall, and I'll belt you right in the mouth . . . Can you imagine me wearing this thing tonight? Of all nights? I mean, I only wear it on special occasions, you know? Some special occasion. At first, earlier this evening, I got all dressed up, my best dress, with matching shoes, pearl earrings, the works. There I was, looking myself over in the full-length mirror, seeing how I looked, and then I realized where I was going. Getting all dressed up to go to an abortion . . . What a stupid life. What a stupid, stupid life.

RANDALL (*Quietly*) Not stupid, atall, little Rosie. Merely somewhat grotesque. You gotta learn to see this here life like in a Coney Island mirror—then you be surprised how all of a sudden everything look perfectly natural.

ROSIE You use your words, Randall, I'll use mine. Stupid.

GLAS Have some coffee.

ROSIE What do you think, Mister Glas? Stupid?

GLAS I have no opinion.

RANDALL Mister Glas a pretty difficult man to pin down, you find. Matter of fact, it been startlin' to me these here past few minutes that he been devotin' any atten-

tion at all to your present predicament. (*To* GLAS) Here
I been thinkin' you to be merely a watcher of the go-by
world, Mister Glas, sir, lackin' the inclination or desire
to be, uh—*involved*.

(*Pause.* GLAS *appears to absorb this without comment; then, when she speaks, turns his attention to*
ROSIE, *who seems lost in thought*)

ROSIE If you knew me better, you'd see that this is exactly
the kind of thing that's likely to happen to me. (*She
resumes the combing of the wig*) Getting knocked up,
I mean. The point is it was my first time, I was a virgin
before that. Wouldn't you know it, I'd get caught? Aside
from everything else, I'm not lucky either. I often think
if I couldn't be beautiful I would've settled for being
lucky. I envy lucky people. My stepfather for instance,
there's a person with luck. Not much brains, but more
luck than you could imagine. He's the type of person
could fall into an open manhole and come up with a
gold watch. You know the type? You see, if I was lucky,
Harold and I could've succumbed to our silly little passion and that would've been that, the end of it. But no,
no such luck. And New Rochelle, of all places. At least
if it'd been in some nice apartment in the Village, say,
with the sounds coming through the window of traffic
and people, the breeze blowing the curtain over the bed,
like in the movies. But, no. I lost my virginity in the
attic of an old house in New Rochelle. Harold's grandmother's house. On a rainy day in spring on the floor of
the attic in his grandmother's house, listening to the rain
on the roof, breathing the dust of old things . . . And
what comes next but his grandmother, who was sup-

posed to be in the city for the day. But instead she's suddenly standing in the door to the attic, attracted there, no doubt, by the scuffling sounds of the imminent consummation. So she's standing there, screaming: Stop that! Stop that this instant! Picture it if you will. Needless to say, it was out of the question. Stopping. At that particular moment. I mean, sex is like a flight over the sea, one reaches the point of no return . . . I guess it sounds funny now but, you know, at the time . . . it was pretty rotten. Sordid, I mean . . . it wasn't at all the way it's supposed to be. And Harold, of all people. A girl finds herself in this predicament, this condition, she'd at least like to be able to think of the cause of it as being some clever, handsome guy with charm and experience who wears Harris tweed sports jackets and tapered slacks, just returned from spending a year in Rome, say, on a Guggenheim fellowship. But, Harold . . . Harold is six foot two, about a hundred and twenty-five pounds, tops, an Economics major at CCNY, he wears blue serge suits about a size too big. I used to be all the time telling him, Harold, why don't you get a suit that fits you? He says it has nothing to do with his suit, it's the way he's built . . . That's about the best I'll ever be able to do, I know it. (*She smiles and snorts*) Ever since I found out I was pregnant I've been walking around with a face down to here and my mother kept saying, What's the matter with you, anyway? I just don't know what's gotten into you lately. So, finally, I told her: a kid named Harold, as a matter of fact . . . Oh, well, I just keep telling myself: Remember, Rosie, like in the song . . . someday my prince will come . . . Snow White . . .

(*Pause*)

RANDALL   Don't worry, little chick: someday your prince'll come.

ROSIE   Sure, sure.

RANDALL   Besides, you had an experience, you know? Very important for a writer to have experiences.

ROSIE   One swallow doth not a summer make, Randall.

GLAS   You say your mama knows? About this?

ROSIE   Oh, yeah.

GLAS   She knows what you're going to do and she doesn't . . . she doesn't care?

ROSIE   Oh, sure. She cares. Certainly. But she's realistic, I'll say that much for her.

GLAS   And your father too?

ROSIE   Not my father. My stepfather. Yeah, he knows, too. But he more or less takes it as a matter of course, something to be expected where I'm concerned: we don't get along too well. Him, all he really cares about are things like "constantly moving up the salary ladder." That's the way he talks: "constantly moving up the salary ladder." Also, he has this *habit* of looking into his handkerchief after he blows his nose. You know what I mean? It's little things like that can really turn you against a person. He's only been married to my mother two years now and they still spend a lot of time just lying around contemplating each other's navels. So, of course, he says my trouble is I'm jealous of my mother and that I wouldn't be so jealous except a lot of my Oedipal conflicts haven't been resolved. I retaliate by accusing him of secretly reading the book reviews in *Time* magazine. I've dis-

77

covered that to be about the most insulting thing I can say to him. Still, he's brought my mother and me a long way up in the world, relatively speaking: from the lower Bronx to Riverdale. I have to grant him that. My real father is dead, you see.

GLAS Ah. I'm sorry to hear.

ROSIE Thank you, yeah, some island out in the middle of the Pacific Ocean. (*Wryly*) Remember that war they had?

GLAS I remember several.

ROSIE Yeah. So Harvey Kasner, age nineteen, gets killed on a stupid sunny day on some stupid island out in the middle of the Pacific Ocean, nineteen forty-three. I would like to've known Harvey Kasner, my mother says he was a pretty nice kid. He never even knew I existed. The letter my mother wrote to tell him she was going to have me came back. He was dead before it got there, it came back unopened with the rest of his stuff, personal effects.

GLAS Mm.

ROSIE And for what! After all the noise dies down and the dead are buried, the politicians come out from under the rocks and split the take. What're your politics now, Mister Glas?

GLAS Hm?

ROSIE Your politics. What are they now?

GLAS I have no politics.

ROSIE Ah. Uh-huh.

GLAS Why do you ask?

78

ROSIE (*Seemingly in a single breath*) Well, that's part of the paper I'm doing, my thesis: the present political affiliations of former concentration camp inmates. I mean, it's one thing to quote hate the Nazis unquote, fairly simple and undemanding. It's something else, though, what one does with that hate, how one channelizes it, politically, with a view to preventing a Nazi ideology or anything resembling it to enjoy a resurgence, a return to power. You'd be surprised to know how many survivors of the camps are essentially apolitical. Not merely unregistered with a particular political party, but in their very thoughts, apolitical.

RANDALL (*To* GLAS) Man! She somethin' *else*, ain't she? (*To* ROSIE) You are somethin' *else*, little chick. Indeed.

ROSIE What does that mean, I'm something else?

RANDALL Well, *you* know . . . it kinda hard to explain . . . somethin' *special*, it means. You know? Somethin' extraordinary.

(*Pause*)

ROSIE Oh.

ROSIE (*To* GLAS) Anyway, that's what I've found to be true among those *I've* interviewed. (*A very brief pause before she turns to* RANDALL, *curiously, with caution and hope*) What do you mean, extraordinary? What's so extraordinary about *me*?

RANDALL Oh, man, *you* know . . . *Style*, Rosie! You got *style*!

ROSIE (*Contemptuously*) Style! This isn't style! This is *front*! All front! But you hit it right on the head, Randall. A style is what you need in this life. You have to find a style and stick to it. That's my whole problem: I haven't been able to find a style yet. What's your style?

RANDALL Oh well, *you* know: a little bit a this, a little bit a that.

(*He exchanges a glance with* GLAS)

ROSIE Forget it! Consistency is *all*!

GLAS You seem to me like you got a very definite style, Rosie.

ROSIE (*Vehemently*) No! Don't you hear what I'm saying? This isn't *style,* it's *front*! But that's what happens, you see: very often front is mistaken for style. No . . . style is . . . something else.

RANDALL We right back where we started.

ROSIE No, I don't mean it the way you meant it. (*To* GLAS) You know Jean Arthur? I met someone who met her once.

GLAS Who.

ROSIE A friend of my stepfather's.

GLAS (*Confused*) Ah. Met whom?

ROSIE Jean Arthur.

GLAS I don't know who that is.

ROSIE Don't you watch the old movies on TV?

GLAS I got no TV, no.

ROSIE Ah. Well, then, you wouldn't know who Jean Arthur was. I mean, she wasn't exactly beautiful either, you know, in the conventional sense, but style—wow!— what a style. Just as a for instance, I mean. But I don't want to get started on movies. If anything ever destroyed the youth of America, it's the movies. I used to be a big movie fan when I was a kid, four, five movies a week. Not any more. I finally saw through them. I finally saw what a hoax and a fraud they really are.

GLAS   I don't go to the movies only once in a while so I don't know.

ROSIE   Take my word for it: lies, all lies. Gene Kelly dancing all over the streets in the pouring rain. Hah! Boy, oh, boy. Between the movies and the myths and slogans you bring us up on, we haven't got a chance.

GLAS   Who.

ROSIE   Us! The children of America! You bring us up on myths and slogans and phony movies and expect us to go out into the world with some style! I mean, myths and slogans, all they leave us with is *front!* (*To* RANDALL) Right? (*She gives him no time to respond*) Sure! So here I am: *all front.* (*A brief pause. She catches her breath and sighs*) Well, at least I don't laugh at everyone's jokes any more. I used to laugh at everyone's jokes, you know. Funny or not.

GLAS   Why.

ROSIE   So they'd like me.

GLAS   Really?

ROSIE   It's nice to be liked.

GLAS   By whom?

ROSIE   Anyone.

GLAS   Did it work?

81

ROSIE What?

GLAS Laughing at everybody's jokes. Did it work? Did they like you?
(*Pause*)

ROSIE (*Thoughtfully*) I don't know, they didn't say. (*Pause*) Anyway, I don't do that any more.

GLAS If I was to make a joke and you didn't laugh that would be okay, I like you anyway.

RANDALL You have captured Mister Glas's heart, little pussycat. Which is no mean trick, I can assure you, indeed. Like I been tryin' alla my life.

ROSIE You know each other a long time, huh?

GLAS I know him about an hour.

ROSIE Oh.
(*Confused, she looks to* RANDALL)

RANDALL Skip it, Rosie. That were merely a private little joke, understood only by me, the significance of which would be somewhat obscure to others, I admit. He's right. He knows me about a hour. Howsomever— (*To* GLAS) "I do desire we may be better strangers." (*To* ROSIE) You know who said that?

ROSIE (*Shakes her head*) You do seem to be unusually well read.
(*Pause*)

RANDALL (*With a sudden edge*) You mean, for, uh— someone like me?

ROSIE What?

RANDALL *You* know: unusual you mean for a young chap of my color and station in life?

ROSIE Your color! Who said anything about your *color?* Listen, buster, you could be yellow polka dots for all I care one way or another. All I said was—

RANDALL We do seem to be comin' up with some *unusual* alternate color schemes this evenin'.

ROSIE I don't know what that's supposed to mean, all I said was—

RANDALL Mister Glas's color scheme was, I think, uh, purple with orange stripes, which also has its points.

ROSIE (*To* GLAS) What's he talking about, do *you* know?

GLAS Don't pay any attention to him.

RANDALL (*Violently*) Now you knock that off, you hear! Knock that off about not payin' any attention! Knock it off! And you! (*He wheels on* ROSIE) Don't you be askin' *him* what I'm talkin' about! You ask *me* what I'm talkin' about! Hear? I be glad to explain it to you, but you ask *me!*

ROSIE (*Unintimidated*) What are you getting so excited about! All I said—

GLAS All right, wait a *minute*, wait a *minute!* (*Silence. All are still*) Everybody relax and be nice. No trouble.

RANDALL (*Quietly*) Mister Glas, sir, you got a absolutely *morbid* fear of trouble, ain'tcha. (*To* ROSIE) I don't need nobody doin' any explainin' for me, little chick. I don't need nobody doin' *nothin'* for me. You dig? (*No response from* ROSIE. *She only returns his gaze steadily*) You dig?

83

GLAS Tell him all right, Rosie. (ROSIE *looks at* GLAS, *then back to* RANDALL) Tell him all right, Rosie.

ROSIE (*Finally*) All right, Randall. (RANDALL *relents and the tension leaves him.* ROSIE'S *attention remains fixed on him, nevertheless, as he begins concentratedly to clean his glasses*) I didn't mean to insult you or anything like that, Randall. It might have sounded patronizing but I didn't mean it that way, honestly.

RANDALL (*With a beaming, totally insincere smile*) Tha's okay, little chick, tha's okay. We jus' drop the whole matter, right?
>   (*Pause.* ROSIE *gazes at him*)

ROSIE (*Coldly*) Listen, you nervy bastard, who do you think you are?

RANDALL Say again?

ROSIE (*Furious*) Giving *me* that Uncle Tom shuffle-and-smile routine?

GLAS (*Apprehensive*) Rosie ...
>   (RANDALL'S *smile fades to one of more natural proportions*)

ROSIE Talk about insulting! I just apologize for sounding patronizing and you come right back and patronize *me*? Who do you think you are!

GLAS Listen, Rosie ...

RANDALL (*His voice normal*) Well, if the truth be told, Rosie, I haven't quite decided yet.
>   (ROSIE *opens her mouth to speak but closes it again. Pause*)

ROSIE What did you say?

RANDALL I said, I haven't quite decided yet. I am, however, working on it constantly.
(ROSIE *nods. Pause*)

ROSIE What's the idea, Randall?

RANDALL Would you care to explain it to her, Mister Glas?

GLAS (*Flatly*) Sometimes he runs out of gas.
(*She waits for some elaboration of that cryptic remark, but none comes*)

ROSIE As an explanation that leaves a lot to be desired. (*To* RANDALL) What's with you, you get your kicks going around putting people on?

RANDALL If I disguise my voice to speak the truth, Rosie, it is no less the truth.

ROSIE (*Drily*) Who said that. (RANDALL *places his hand gently upon his breast. He turns and exits.* ROSIE *looks after him in silence for a moment. He reappears in the store as* ROSIE *turns to* GLAS) What's the idea with him?

GLAS It's a long story.
(*The lights fade on the kitchen while, in the store,* RANDALL *moves to the street door and stands, looking out into the darkness. He begins to hum the tune again: "No Hiding Place." The lights fade to black*)

Scene Two

The lights rise again on the store. The kitchen remains dark. Some minutes have elapsed. RANDALL *is as before, gazing into the street. In the hallway door* ROSIE *stands, very still, watching him. He seems to become aware of her presence, turns, looks at her, then turns again to the street. After a moment, he moves away, slowly, and comes to rest upon a stool at the counter, his face vacant, his attitude detached, impassive. Slowly, he removes his cape, his hat, his glasses and places them on the counter.*

RANDALL   Where is our good Samaritan?
> *(Throughout, now, except where otherwise indicated,* RANDALL's *voice and actions are natural, the parody is gone)*

ROSIE *(With a vague gesture toward the apartment)* I don't know, feeding the goldfish, or something. *(She smiles;* RANDALL *smiles)* No, actually, he's washing the dishes.

RANDALL   Fastidious.

ROSIE   Yeah.

RANDALL   He's afraid of me, you know, our Mister Glas.

ROSIE   Why do you say that? *(No response to this from* RANDALL. ROSIE *places her handbag and wig on the counter)* He's been telling me about you.

RANDALL   He knows little.

86

ROSIE Very interesting, though. I mean, do you really have an IQ of a hundred and eighty-seven?

RANDALL So they tell me.

ROSIE That's some fantastic IQ.

RANDALL You're envious, Rosie?

ROSIE Well, not envious exactly. I wouldn't mind having a mind like that, though. I mean, with a mind like that one could do anything. You. You could do great things.

RANDALL (*Already anticipating the answer*) For whom?

ROSIE Well . . . for anyone. For your race, for one thing. Certainly for your race. (RANDALL *smiles, having gotten the answer*) You don't agree?

RANDALL You're a splendid girl, Rosie. A little on the square side, but a splendid girl.

ROSIE Why. What's square about that?

RANDALL I'm a freak, Rosie. You've heard the expression: In the country of the blind the one-eyed man is king? (*He shakes his head*) In the country of the blind the one-eyed man is a freak.

ROSIE Depends on how you look at it.

RANDALL Through my single, freak's eye.

ROSIE Exactly. A partial vision, Randall.

RANDALL But the only one available to me. What else did he tell you?

87

ROSIE Oh . . . that you don't have any place to live and
that you've been in trouble with the police and that you
have some kind of heart condition and about your mother
being a . . . well, about your mother.

RANDALL Prostitute.

ROSIE Yes.

RANDALL I thought you were unafraid of the right words,
Rosie. (*Mimicking her, but kindly*) Prostitute! See? The
roof didn't fall in. (*He grins; she returns it*) What else.

ROSIE What?

RANDALL What else did he tell you?

ROSIE Well . . . that you're probably in trouble right now.
(RANDALL *smiles*) That you were running away from
something when you came in here tonight. (RANDALL
nods) You were?

RANDALL I was acknowledging the information, not ad-
mitting to the charge.

ROSIE Oh. Well, *are* you in some kind of trouble?
(*Pause*)

RANDALL When are you going to start writing your books,
Rosie?
(*Pause. She acknowledges the evasion with a wry
smile and is prepared to submit to it for the moment,
but her question remains unanswered and her eyes
never leave him*)

ROSIE I've already started.

RANDALL Ah?

ROSIE I've begun my first novel.

RANDALL Well, now. What's it about?

ROSIE I don't know yet.

RANDALL You've already begun it and you don't know what it's about?

ROSIE I'll find out as I move along.

RANDALL Ah. Well, what's the title to be?

ROSIE It doesn't have one yet.

RANDALL Ah. Well, I'll be sure to keep my eyes open for a book written by Rosie Kasner.

ROSIE Rosalind.

RANDALL Hm?

ROSIE My full name is Rosalind.

RANDALL Oh. That's a nice name, Rosalind. Rosie's a nice name, but Rosalind is nicer. Beautiful, actually. You ought to call yourself Rosalind.

ROSIE (*Snorts*) Open your eyes, Randall. Do I look like a Rosalind?

RANDALL What does a Rosalind look like?
(*A pause; finally, her eyes leave him*)

ROSIE (*Dreamily*) Ohhh . . . like the early Katharine Hepburn, maybe. (RANDALL *smiles, unseen by* ROSIE) I wish I was beautiful to match my beautiful name.

(RANDALL *snatches up the wig, puts it on and postures, an attempt to distract her from thoughts of absent beauty*)

RANDALL   Hey! Do I look like a Rosalind?

ROSIE (*Drily*)   You look like a colored queen.

RANDALL (*Removing the wig, and in the dialect*)   Least I don't have *that* problem. Gotta be thankful for small favors, like they say. (*Then, naturally*) Do you want to know a secret, as a matter of fact?

ROSIE   About what.

RANDALL   About me.

ROSIE   What.

RANDALL   I'm a virgin, as a matter of fact.
(*Pause*)

ROSIE   Oh?

RANDALL (*Nods*)   I've been saving it all up.

ROSIE (*Apprehensively*)   I beg your pardon?

RANDALL   I've been saving it all up.

ROSIE   Saving what all up?

RANDALL   My passion.

ROSIE   Oh . . . Really? Well . . . that's very interesting, isn't it.

RANDALL   Why.

ROSIE Well, because . . . I don't know, it's . . . well, I guess it's not really all *that* interesting, I just meant . . . Well, Jesus, *I* don't know! What do you mean, *why!* What are you telling *me* for?

RANDALL (*After a brief pause*) I thought it would be interesting. In the meantime, I had been studying up on it.

ROSIE On what.

RANDALL The Art. The Art of Love. You know: the uses of the flesh.

ROSIE Studying up?

RANDALL Many books on that subject now. And when the time were to come, what a truly cataclysmic explosion of Love it would be! . . . But it looks as though the matter will end this way.

ROSIE What way?

RANDALL That I will end a stranger to the ways and uses of the flesh, Rosie.

ROSIE Why.

RANDALL No hiding place, Rosie.

ROSIE What?

RANDALL My soul is corrupt, Rosie, but, O, my flesh is pure.

ROSIE What are you talking about, Randall?
     (GLAS *appears at the door*)

RANDALL I'm still here, Mister Glas.

GLAS   So I see.
(*He moves into the room*)

RANDALL   I'll go if you want me to go.

GLAS   Yeah, sure.

RANDALL   Truly.
(*Pause.* GLAS *regards him for a moment*)

GLAS (*Turning away*)   Go, stay, it makes no difference to me.

RANDALL   Actually, I find myself suddenly very tired and would very much like to sit quietly for a bit. What are *your* immediate plans, Rosie?

GLAS   You finally decided to talk right and stop with the funny stuff, hah?

ROSIE   Yeah, why *do* you do that, Randall?

RANDALL   I don't know.

ROSIE (*Impatiently*)   Well, you *must know*.

RANDALL   Why.

ROSIE (*Annoyed*)   Oh, come on.

RANDALL (*In the dialect*)   You a college-educated person, little Rosie, why not *you* tell *me*? You could write us a watchamacallit, a thesis on it, even.
(*Pause*)

ROSIE   You win.

GLAS   He always wins.

RANDALL   Do you really want to know? (ROSIE *gazes at him, wanting to know*) It is my what you might call insulation against the fire of life. (*He smiles*) Mister Glas spells his name with one s, did you know that? German for the glass with two esses.

ROSIE   That's an exciting bit of information.

RANDALL   Well, I only wanted to be sure you spelled it right in your thesis on camp survivors.

GLAS (*Alerted*)   What?

ROSIE   No, I'm not—

RANDALL (*To* GLAS)   I said I wanted to be sure she spelled your name correctly in her thesis.

GLAS   Wait a minute, no name, you don't use my name, you know.

ROSIE   Of course not. (*To* RANDALL) What are you getting everybody excited for? (*To* GLAS) I don't use anyone's name, Mister Glas. Of course not. (*To* RANDALL) What are you trying to do, make trouble or something?

RANDALL   Why don't you want her to use your name, Mister Glas?

ROSIE   I *don't use names*. Will you stop?

RANDALL   What *is* your story, Mister Glas?

GLAS   What story?

RANDALL   Who you are: *that* story.

GLAS   I thought you said you were very tired and wanted to sit quiet for a while? So why don't you sit quiet for a while?

RANDALL   There are many people in this world, Rosie, with a Do Not Disturb sign hung around their necks. Invisible, but present. Mister Glas is one of those. "Among wolves one must howl a little," Mister Glas. Have you ever heard that? (*No answer from* GLAS. *He turns to* ROSIE) Have you ever heard that, Rosie? (*She nods*) Do you know who said it, Rosie?

ROSIE   Voltaire, wasn't it?

RANDALL   Are you asking me or telling me, Rosie?

ROSIE   Voltaire.

RANDALL   Yes. The point is Mister Glas has never learned to howl. You see? He has no talent for it, you see? The wolves are howling their heads off out there and Mister Glas is in here keeping his trap strictly shut. (*Turns to* GLAS) True, Mister Glas? (GLAS *stares at him*) Why, Mister Glas?

GLAS   I told you why already once.

RANDALL   To watch the world go by and keep out of its way? That's no answer, Mister Glas. Survival. That's why, Mister Glas.

ROSIE   I don't follow this at all.

RANDALL   You came in late, Rosie, and there's no second showing of this feature, you'll have to fill in the gaps for yourself.

ROSIE   Thanks a lot.

RANDALL   Survival, Mister Glas? True?

GLAS   You said yourself, they kill you out there.

RANDALL   But survival is possible for a time even out there, Mister Glas. Behold Randall: *I* survive.

GLAS   With an ice pick? With a gun?

ROSIE   *What* ice pick.

RANDALL   One chooses ones means, Mister Glas.

ROSIE   *What* gun.

RANDALL   We're all going to fall on the killing ground one day or another, Mister Glas. At least, I'll die in action. And it's you who has the gun, remember? You're in no position to look with contempt upon those of us who choose to defend ourselves: it's *you* who has the gun.
(GLAS *reaches below the counter, comes up with the revolver in his hand and throws it with contempt onto the counter.* ROSIE, *of course, is startled*)

GLAS   Empty.
(*Pause*)

RANDALL   Empty?
(GLAS *picks up the gun, holding it by the barrel*)

GLAS   To frighten someone who means me harm, maybe, yes. To kill with, never.
(*He drops the gun again on the counter.* RANDALL *smiles, takes up the gun, gazes at it*)

ROSIE   What the hell *is* this?

RANDALL   Haven't you ever heard the rule, Mister Glas? Never point an unloaded gun at anyone?

ROSIE   You mean a loaded gun. What—

95

RANDALL   You're not catching up fast enough, Rosie, the plot is getting away from you. (*Quickly to* GLAS *before she can reply*) You take a terrible chance, Mister Glas. To threaten with this—you could be a dead man.

ROSIE   Listen—

RANDALL   Before—when you asked me to empty the gun—what was that?

GLAS   A little joke on you.
(RANDALL *places the gun on the counter*)

RANDALL   You fascinate me, Mister Glas. From the start here tonight, you've fascinated me.

GLAS   (*Returning the gun to its place beneath the counter*) I got a fascinating personality.

RANDALL   You also confuse me, of course.

GLAS   So you said.

ROSIE   Would someone explain to me what exactly is going on here?
(*Pause.* RANDALL *gazes at her*)

RANDALL   Rosie, if I were dying right now would you save my life?
(*A short pause*)

ROSIE   *I* don't know. Maybe, if I could. Why.

RANDALL   How far would you go? To what extent?

ROSIE   How far would I *have* to go?

RANDALL   Would you die *for* me? Would you go that far?
(*Pause*)

96

ROSIE No.

RANDALL Why not.

GLAS There was only one Jesus Christ, sonny.

RANDALL And they don't make them like *that* any more, Mister Glas, sir. (*To* ROSIE) But you'd try, then, hm?

ROSIE Try what.

RANDALL To save my *life*. If I were *dying*.

GLAS Don't play with her, Randall.

ROSIE (*Cautiously*) Yes, I'd try.

RANDALL Take a good look at me, Rosie. (*He waits*) Are you looking?

ROSIE Of course I'm looking.

RANDALL All right, I'm dying. Save me.
(*Pause*)

ROSIE I don't understand.

GLAS Leave her alone, Randall. (*To* ROSIE) Randall has done some terrible thing tonight, Rosie.

ROSIE (*Alarmed*) What has he done?

GLAS I don't know. Some terrible thing.

ROSIE Randall? What have you done?
(*No response from* RANDALL)

GLAS The police are after him, perhaps. Or someone else. But, whoever it is will kill him for what he has done.

ROSIE Kill him?

RANDALL I've known from the very first instant, Mister Glas, that we—understood. Each other.

GLAS I can't save you. A little bit, maybe, like before with the cops. But finally—no.
(*Pause.* RANDALL *flings himself away*)

RANDALL (*In the dialect*) 'Course you can't! Tha's a *dream*! I have alla my life been buildin' castles inside-a my skull and fillin' them with dreamed people . . . livin' dreamed lives . . . and in my castles there is no death . . .

ROSIE What is it you've done, Randall?

RANDALL How do *you* feel about death, Rosie?

ROSIE (*Drily*) I'm against it. (*Pause.* RANDALL *gazes at her, waiting for a true answer.* GLAS *appears to be deeply absorbed in some private thought of his own*) Well, if you really want to know, I can't conceive of death. Death is not-feeling, I can't conceive of not-feeling. Those people who donate their bodies to science after they're dead? I could never do that. They'd come at my dead body with a knife and I'd *feel* it, I *know* I would.

RANDALL I might have known your attitude would be a unique one, Rosie.

ROSIE Not very realistic, is it.

RANDALL Dead is dead, Rosie, and only then the knife holds no pain.

ROSIE What is it you've done, Randall?

RANDALL Hm?

ROSIE Don't be evasive, Randall. You're in trouble, right?

98

RANDALL   You're the one in trouble, Rosie.

ROSIE   Me?

RANDALL   In trouble. To use the idiomatic phraseology.

ROSIE   Oh. That. My trouble is easily fixed.

RANDALL (*Touching the point of his umbrella to her abdomen*) With the knife you dread so much.
(*A pause. She backs away from the umbrella*)

ROSIE   What is it you've done, Randall?

RANDALL (*In the dialect*)   Sweety, I'm what the psychologists call a "unreachable youth." You tryin' to reach me?

GLAS   Don't tease her, Randall.
(*He speaks quietly, without looking at them. He has been listening, apparently, but for how long we cannot tell*)

ROSIE   It's all right, I'm used to it. (*To* RANDALL) You don't want to pursue this then, right?

RANDALL   No.

ROSIE   I always take no for an answer.

RANDALL   A defeatist attitude, Rosie.

ROSIE   Just don't forget I offered.

GLAS   Don't be offended, Rosie. There's nothing you could do for him. And he knows it.

ROSIE   How do you *know* there's nothing I could do for him? (*To* RANDALL) How do you *know*?

RANDALL   What could you do, Rosie? Give me a for instance.

ROSIE   Well . . . Well, I don't know! I could give you an alibi! I could do that!

RANDALL   An alibi for what?

ROSIE   For whatever it is you've done, goddamnit. What do you think for what?

RANDALL   How do you know I've done anything?

ROSIE   You just said you did!

RANDALL   This gentleman here said I did.

ROSIE   You agreed with him!

RANDALL   Mister Glas, did I agree with you?

GLAS   Leave her alone, Randall! (*Exploding*) LEAVE HER ALONE, NOW!

ROSIE   Oh, forget it!

GLAS   (*Violently*)   What kind of books are you going to write, Rosie! Books about how people save each other's lives, I bet! Don't you believe it, Rosie! Nobody saves nobody! Right, Randall?

RANDALL   An indisputable truth.

ROSIE   (*To* RANDALL) That's one hell of an attitude! (*To* GLAS) Just because *you* don't care?

GLAS   You want to save somebody, Rosie? (*Pointing to her abdomen*) Save *that* life, then! Save what you *can* save!

ROSIE Shut up about that! We're not talking about that!

GLAS No?

ROSIE What do you know about it!
(*She turns away, quickly, holding herself, protecting herself*)

GLAS *I* know! *I* know!

RANDALL (*Quietly*) What do you know, Mister Glas, sir?

GLAS (*After a pause, quietly*) *I* know.

RANDALL Of course you do, we know that. But what, exactly? (*He grins*) Your turn to speak, Mister Glas . . . our turn to listen.
(*A long pause.* RANDALL *waits, watching* GLAS. GLAS *returns his gaze, then looks to* ROSIE, *who, still angry, is turned away; he looks again to* RANDALL. *Finally, his gaze shifts from* RANDALL, *he takes up the newspaper from the counter-top, looks at the headline*)

GLAS This man . . . Do you know what they say? They say that when they arrested him he appeared to be relieved. Not frightened. Not angry. Not defiant. They say he appeared to be—*relieved!* . . . Do you know why? I'll tell you why. Because all these years he knew, you see. He waited, and he knew that sooner or later it would happen: the discovery that would mean his judgment and his death. And the anticipation of a blow is always, somehow, more terrible than the blow itself when it finally comes. So, one can understand his relief. When the blow finally came.

ROSIE (*Hostile*) He doesn't deserve anything so comforting as relief. He deserves what he got.

RANDALL (*Quietly, his eyes on* GLAS) Bloodthirsty, Rosie.

ROSIE When it comes to the Eichmanns of this world I get very Jewish. (*To* GLAS) I should think you'd feel the same.

RANDALL (*His eyes still on* GLAS, *waiting*) Mister Glas isn't a Jew.

GLAS But I had a wife who was a Jew. And a son who was a Jew—for his mother's sake. Ten years old he was then. Nineteen thirty-eight. To be married to a Jew in Germany in nineteen thirty-eight, Rosie, a man might as well have been a Jew himself: the Nazis made no distinctions. But you probably know that, you're an educated girl. And, of course, to have been a Jew then was to wait for the day they opened your door and took you away. They opened so many doors . . . so many doors . . . and came out with Jews in their fists . . . Most men, you know, most men can live all of their lives with the conviction that they have honor, and they can go to their graves with that conviction without ever having been put to the test of it. I envy them, the ones who escape the test. Not me. In the summer of nineteen thirty-eight I had my test, my choice to make: to wait until I was taken to a concentration camp as a Jew with my Jewish wife and my Jewish son . . . or to live as a Communist and fight for my country, my Germany, against the Nazis. Sure, you can say: Where is the choice there, where is the choice to make against loyalty to your wife, to your son? Easy to say. Even for me, easy to say now.

But not then. Because, you see, the Party was above all, belief in the Party transcended all morality. Of course, this is impossible to believe, I know, for anyone who was not of it. But it was true: the Party was God, the defeat of Nazism our Paradise to be attained on earth, our German earth. And, to save my life for that fight, I abandoned them, my wife and my child, in the middle of a night, without a word. I went to another city, I took another name. All for the Party, for the glorious cause. I was a railroad engineer in those days, and the war was coming, and the trains were rolling day and night in Germany then, day and night. For nearly a year I carried freight between Hamburg and Cologne: chemicals, machinery, armaments. From time to time I would get news of home, from comrades, that my wife and son were well, were safe yet. And this made it a little easier for me to live, to work for the cause, for the dream . . . And then I was transferred to another run, to a place called Mauthausen, and the freight was people . . . People . . . Oh yes, I might have refused such a job. Of course. But to refuse would have been suspect. They would investigate the man who made such a protest, they would surely discover me to be a Communist, they would imprison me. And to be imprisoned then would have made meaningless the abandonment of my wife and my child and that *had* to have meaning, do you see, it *had* to! . . . So I did not refuse, I did not protest . . . Three trips I made in two months and I carried hundreds and hundreds of people, Jews, to the concentration camp at Mauthausen. They herded them along the platform away from the train and I never looked at them, I turned away and closed my eyes and tried to think of

103

other things. Like the necessary evils we must sometimes do for the sake of a higher *good*, a nobler *cause*. In the history of the world, what dreadful deeds have been done under the protection of that dreadful idea . . . Until August, nineteen thirty-nine, and Stalin made his pact with Hitler. Communism embraced Nazism, my god kissed Satan and called him friend. In that moment there was a new truth: that I had abandoned my wife and my son to the wolves and saved myself for nothing. For *nothing*! My life, without them, had been without meaning. And their death without me, when it came, would be equally without meaning. Unless . . . unless, it was not too late, hah? Of course! I could go back! With what dignity and honor there was left to me! I could go back to my wife—whether she would forgive me or not, whether she would have me or not. I would live with her again, and with my son, as the husband of a Jew, as the father of a Jew, and wait for them to open our door and take us! . . . Together . . . And I went back . . . and in the house the windows were smashed . . . and the door was open . . . and they were gone. (*Pause*) I left Germany then. (*Pause*) Save what you *can* save, Rosie. I know.

ROSIE (*Ignoring this, perhaps not hearing it; quietly*) You were never in a concentration camp. (*Silence from* GLAS) Your arm, the number.

GLAS   A tattoo fellow did it for me. Here in Brooklyn.

ROSIE   But, *why*?

GLAS   I don't know . . . It was *supposed* to be there, it *should* have happened . . . Do you understand?

RANDALL (*Without looking at* GLAS) The leg, Mister Glas? That they were supposed to have broken up?

GLAS A railroad accident.

RANDALL And the stories about the camp you were supposed to have been in?

GLAS Everyone knows those stories. They are all true. Not my truth . . . but the truth.

ROSIE Jesus.

GLAS (*Taking up the newspaper*) For this man . . . the waiting is over. He committed a crime for which a punishment has been named, you see. But me. Who will judge *me*? Who will condemn *me*, and by what law? (*He moves to the door, opens it, looks out into the street*) The first time I told my truth in twenty-three years.

RANDALL (*With irony*) The truth shall make you free, Mister Glas.

> (GLAS *looses a cry of anguish into the street. He moves out. After a moment,* ROSIE *moves to the door. Pause*)

RANDALL What is he doing?

ROSIE Sitting on the curb.

RANDALL Mm.

ROSIE Randall?

RANDALL Mm?

ROSIE I think he's crying.

RANDALL Mm, hm.

ROSIE Yes, he is. He's crying. (RANDALL *takes up the wig from the counter-top*) Shouldn't we do something?

RANDALL (*His attention on the wig*) You amaze me, Rosie, you truly do. You always think there's something to be *done*.
>   (*He puts on the wig, unseen by* ROSIE, *who is still at the door, looking out*)

ROSIE Jesus.

RANDALL Mourn not, little Rosie, mourn not. (*He moves to the juke box, inserts a coin in the slot; the machine comes alive in colored lights*) Maybe we'll think of something, Rosie.

ROSIE (*Without turning*) What?

RANDALL I said: maybe we'll think of something. To be *done*.
>   (*He is studying his reflection in the glass of the juke box when the record begins: it is the voice of Frank Sinatra singing "You Go to My Head."* RANDALL *remains at the machine,* ROSIE *at the door. At the end of the first few bars of the song the curtain falls on Act Two. The music continues behind the curtain, and fades out slowly as the house lights come up*)

Act Three

Coda

ACT THREE

Before the rise, the music is again heard, continuing. At the rise, the scene is revealed as before; several moments have elapsed. ROSIE *is still at the door,* RANDALL *at the juke box. The last few bars of the song are sung, the record ends. Silence.* ROSIE *turns from the door and moves, despondently, to a stool and sits, having glanced only briefly at* RANDALL.

ROSIE   You look ridiculous.

RANDALL (*Absently*)   Hmmm?

ROSIE   Will you take the wig off, this is hardly the time for jokes. (RANDALL, *still absorbed, takes the wig from his head*) I feel very sorry for him, Randall.

RANDALL   You do seem to be missing the point, sweet Rosie. He doesn't want you to feel *sorry* for him, he doesn't want your *pity*. Save your pity for those who want it, Rosie, don't piddle it away on those who don't.

ROSIE (*A rhetorical question*)   Well, what are you supposed to do, a man dumps a story like that right in your lap?
　　　(*Pause*)

RANDALL   Stand up.

ROSIE   Haven't you any compassion at *all*?

RANDALL (*With mock interest*)   What is that: compassion.

ROSIE   Up yours.

RANDALL   Promise? (*She makes a gesture of annoyance and dismissal and moves again to the door, looking out*) I mean, that compassion, that's okay up to a point, little Rosie, that's what you do until the doctor comes, but it doesn't do much good, you know, finally.

ROSIE   I suppose not.

RANDALL   So I suppose it's time we did something, then.

ROSIE   About what.

RANDALL   Him.

ROSIE   What can we do? You said yourself—

RANDALL   He still there?

ROSIE   Yes. (RANDALL *moves to the ladder, drags it noisily to the center of the room*) Now what.

RANDALL   You said what could we do, Rosie, and I said perhaps we'll think of something.

ROSIE   So?

RANDALL   So, I've thought of something and we'll do it, then.

ROSIE   What.

RANDALL   Mister Glas is a victim of every man's unfortunate need to be judged, Rosie.
        (*He moves a stool to a point several feet in front of the ladder*)

ROSIE   So?

RANDALL   So, we'll do that little thing, Rosie.

ROSIE   What little thing?

RANDALL   (*Offering his hand*)   Be seated, Rosie, be seated.

ROSIE   What?

RANDALL   Sit. Here.

ROSIE   What the hell for? What are you doing, anyway?
(*He takes her by the hand, leads her to the counter, lifts
her, and seats her on it*) Now, listen, Randall—!

RANDALL   Ssh!
(*He moves about the store, pulling the light cords,
leaving, finally, only a single light burning. It illu-
minates, in a circle of light, the area around the
ladder, the stool, and* ROSIE *on the counter. He puts
on his cape and ascends the ladder with* ROSIE's *wig
in his hand.* ROSIE *is fascinated, but still annoyed.*
RANDALL *sits on the very top of the ladder and
ceremoniously dons the wig*)

ROSIE   What exactly is this game called?

RANDALL   It has no name, I just invented it. It's the game
without a name.

ROSIE   Okay, I'll bite. What now?

RANDALL   We wait. For the principal party in these proceedings.
(*On cue,* GLAS *appears in the doorway*)

GLAS   What's going on?

111

RANDALL Short wait.
(*There is a change in* GLAS: *his erect carriage is no more, he is hunched, slumped. It is as though his secret had been the core of him, the force sustaining him, that which has held him erect. Having divulged his secret at last, the core has been drawn out, the shell is collapsed*)

GLAS What's all this here? (*He moves into the room and stops, unintentionally, within the circle of light, and looking up at* RANDALL) What are you doing up there? Why are the lights out? Rosie, what's this?

ROSIE (*Embarrassed suddenly*) I don't really know, Mister Glas. I'm sorry.
(*She moves as if to leave the counter*)

RANDALL *Sit*, Rosie!
(*She stays*)

ROSIE Listen, you nut—

RANDALL (*In the dialect*) You stand accused, Mister Glas, sir!

GLAS *What, what?*

RANDALL Accused, yes!

ROSIE He's crazy, Mister Glas. I'm convinced.
(*Using the ice pick as a gavel,* RANDALL *pounds on the ladder-top*)

RANDALL (*His voice like a machine gun*) Hear ye! hear ye! God bless all here! We are gathered together here for certain special and particular purposes, to wit: to determine the guilt or innocence on various and particu-

lar charges of one, Glas, first name unknown and immaterial, brought forward here and now before this here
qualified tri-bunal—that's me—with the view in mind to
settin' his heretofore troubled conscience at rest con-
cernin' a certain matter, to wit: his need to be judged.
And perhaps to be condemned, also, but we don't wanta
be gettin' ahead of ourselves. The jury—that's you, Rosie
—havin' already made convincin' prior statements regardin' its concern in and compassion for the accused,
may consider itself duly sworn to consider and ponder
the various ramifications and aspects of the case which
will now be presented before it and to deliver at the
requisite time the proper various verdicts which are
demanded by the laws previously set down by this here
society regardin' the execution of justice in all its forms.

ROSIE Jee*esus.*

RANDALL The jury will refrain from unauthorized com-
ments that tend to disrupt the order of this court. (*To*
GLAS) The defendant will rise. (*He adds, parentheti-
cally*) Tha's okay, it a mere formality, since you already
on your feet. (ROSIE *clicks her tongue, loudly*) The jury
is pushin' for a charge of contempt by this here court
unless it be more circumspect and reserved in its reac-
tions to the procedure herein bein' carried out. Be
warned, jury. (*Returning to* GLAS) The first charge to
be considered before this tri-bunal here convened is that
of, uh—abandonment. Specifically, the abandonment
aforethought of the family of the accused, specifically,
one wife and one son, aged, uh—ten? Yeah, ten years of
age, which act of abandonment was carried out in the
full knowledge of the position in which they—that is,

the wife and son of the accused—was bein' placed,
namely, dire peril of their lives; alone and unprotected;
imminent death; and other inconveniences. How do you
plead? Guilty or not guilty?
(*Pause.* GLAS *stares up at* RANDALL)

ROSIE   Should I call a cop, Mister Glas?
(GLAS *looks at* ROSIE, *the faintest of smiles on his
lips. He still has the smile when, after a moment,
he turns again to* RANDALL, *looks up and speaks
matter-of-factly*)

GLAS   Guilty.

ROSIE   Mister Glas . . . ?

RANDALL   The jury will *refrain!*

ROSIE (*To herself*)   I knew the minute I walked into this
place it was some kind of a nuthouse.

RANDALL   How says the jury? (*Silence.* ROSIE *is gazing at*
GLAS, *who continues to stare at* RANDALL, *the faint smile
still on his lips*) How says the jury!

ROSIE   What?

RANDALL   Guilty or not guilty?

ROSIE   *What?*

RANDALL   The jury must reach a verdict on the charge
herein just enumerated and specified. How do you find
the defendant? Guilty or not guilty? Of the charge of
abandonment?

ROSIE   If I had a mind to, I could point out a very basic
little flaw in this whole farce, you know? The fact is, he

already said he was guilty, so you don't need any opinion from the jury, or whatever it is I'm supposed to be. That's if I had a mind to. Which I haven't.

RANDALL   The accused's own opinion and hearsay evidence is naturally prejudiced and inadmissible for the purposes of this tri-bunal. Guilty or not guilty, jury?

ROSIE   Boy! You sure are hard to—

GLAS   *Say*, Rosie!
(*Pause. She gazes at* GLAS)

ROSIE   You too?

GLAS   (*More quietly*)   Say, Rosie.
(*Pause. She looks at* RANDALL, *at* GLAS *again.* GLAS *waits, staring straight ahead at* RANDALL's *impatiently tapping foot*)

ROSIE   You already said you were guilty. (*To* RANDALL) He already said he did it.

RANDALL   The jury do seem to be losin' sight and grasp of the main issue at hand here. Certainly *he* said it. Nobody *else* said it, however. *Yet.* That the issue at hand which we takin' care of now in this here tri-bunal.

GLAS   (*Still more quietly, insistent*)   Say, Rosie.
(*Pause*)

ROSIE   (*Quietly*)   Guilty, yes. Mister Glas . . . ?

GLAS   (*Without looking at her*)   Ssh, Rosie.
(*He shakes his head*)

RANDALL   Havin' got out of the way that there relative simple aspect of the charges bein' considered here this evenin', we can now proceed to the more difficult and complex matters been laid before this tri-bunal, to wit, and takin' them one step at a time: Matter number one: is this here defendant guilty of a certain what might be called *moral de-formity* currently to be found present in certain types of individuals now resident within the context of this, uh—society that we got goin' for us at the moment. And, matter number two: . . . well, we get to that somewhat later, it bein' perhaps the most, should I say, ticklish specification of, and arisin' directly out of, the general charge, which is, to wit: that of havin' found himself in a *moral dilemma* in the *first* place. Now—

ROSIE   May I ask a question?

RANDALL   A time and place will be set upon the completion of this tri-bunal for the purposes of the askin' and answerin' of questions. All questions regardin' the procedure and operation of this tri-bunal will be deferred until that time. (*Bangs the "gavel"*) Now to consider in more detail this here charge of *moral deformity* which been directed at the accused now before us. You will recall, if you will, the defendant's testimonial that some time after the abandonment of his family, he found himself present in another somewhat tricky situation, to wit: employment as the uh, driver of a train that were engaged in the transport of certain parties, namely the Jews, to the place of their death, that place bein', specifically—and let it be entered into the record of these here proceedings—that place bein' uh . . . uh . . .

ROSIE   Mauthausen.

RANDALL   Correct. Mauthausen. Now. A charge of this here nature naturally raise certain types of questions in the minds of those concerned in the consideration of the defendant's case here before us. Question number one: Did the defendant know—I mean, *know*—whether or not these here parties, namely the Jews, were maybe criminal types convicted by the laws of that time and place of any particular depredations *against* the laws of that time and place? The answer is clear here: no. Definitely. It bein' a matter of record accordin' to the accused's own testimonial that he knew them people to be Jews merely and no criminal types convicted of crimes against the state by due process of law. Correct? Correct. Question number two: Did the accused here before us know the purpose for which the said parties were bein' transported to the place called Mauthausen? Or, to be more and further specific, did he *know*, I mean was he fully *aware*, that the parties were bein' transported to the place of their ultimate and inescapable death? The answer, in the very words of the accused, is yes. Definitely. How do the accused plead? Guilty or not guilty?

GLAS   Guilty.

RANDALL   How do the jury find? (*Silence*) How do the—

ROSIE   Guilty, yes.

RANDALL   We movin' nicely right along here now. (*Bangs the "gavel"*) This bring us to the very brink of that most ticklish aspect of this case which already been alluded to earlier in these proceedings, to wit: the subsequent disposition of the defendant's Self *by* hisself. I perceive a demeanor of confusion and puzzlement on the countenance of the jury which indicate the necessity of some elucidation of the foregoin' statement. To put the matter in terms readily understandable and graspable to all, to wit: Did the accused, upon learnin' of its true nature, *refuse* the employment which tended to incriminate him as a direct accomplice in the unspeakable deaths inflicted upon many hundreds of innocent persons, namely the Jews? Which refusal to cooperate would, in all likelihood, have brought down upon his head exposure of his true political affiliations and ultimate death by execution as a enemy of the State and Constituted Order of that time and place? Did he refuse? He did not. Definitely. On the contrary, jury, *on the contrary.* What he did was, he donned his overhalls and chugged his choo-choo right on inta that place, Mauthausen, keepin' his mouth strictly shut, as we have discovered to be his habit and approach to life. And, subsequent to that, havin' discovered the folly of his ways, which is to say, the folly of his havin' deserted his wife and his child for the sake of a *cause*—to wit: the commonists—the folly of aiding and abetting in the act of murder for the sake of that *cause,* these bein' *discovered* to be follies on the moment of his betrayal by that very same *cause* when it turn right around, somewhat confusingly, and kiss and make up with its up-till-then sworn enemy, the *other* cause, to wit: the Nazis. True, we gotta reserve a little bit a sympathy for the accused at this point 'cause we gotta admit there ain't nothin' quite so upsettin' as discoverin' you been believin' in the *wrong cause.* But that neither here nor there, actually. Or, to be more precise, it *there,* but not *here.* Which bring us back to the original matter under consideration, to wit: the disposition of the defendant's Self *by* hisself upon discoverin' the Folly of his Ways. Did he, in expiation for his crimes, throw hisself beneath the wheels of that very same choo-choo that he'd been runnin' back and forth to the place called Mauthausen? He did not. As is plain to see. *Au contraire*, jury, *au contraire*. He *es-caped*, is what he did. He *withdrew* from the *field* of *battle*. He *lived*.

ROSIE   He tried to go back to his family first.

RANDALL   A gesture which we must be constrained to look upon with caution, jury, if not with outright suspicion. A somewhat *tardy* gesture, if you will, whose outcome was foreordained under the then existing circumstances as explained by the accused hisself, right?

ROSIE   Maybe. Nevertheless.

RANDALL   Let it be entered into the record of these proceedin's then, to be taken under advisement, perhaps, by some higher court in the future to which this case may or may not be appealed. For the purposes of this present tri-bunal the matter is immaterial and irrelevant. (*A crack of the "gavel"*) Therefore. The defendant stands accused of the charge of continuing. Continuing to maintain himself in a aura of public innocence. Continuing not to seek out punishment for his crimes. Continuing, in short, to live. How do you plead?

GLAS   Guilty.

RANDALL   Jury? Guilty or not guilty?

ROSIE   Of what.

RANDALL   Of *continuing*, jury. To *live*.

ROSIE   Well, he's alive, isn't he?

RANDALL   The jury will be bound by the uses of the proper and prescribed terminology herein required by this court. Guilty or not guilty, jury?

ROSIE   Guilty.

RANDALL   The jury havin' voiced no dissent with, and bein' in agreement with, the judgment of the defendant —and also, I might add, with the privately held and hitherto undivulged opinions of this court, namely me— all that bein' the case, this court find the defendant guilty on all counts here before it this evenin' and, havin' no alternative, do sentence the defendant to death in the first degree. Done. *Done*, then!
   (*A crack of the "gavel."* RANDALL *descends the ladder and drives the point of the ice pick into the counter-top. He leaps, in a slow, graceful handspring, over the counter. He takes the gun from its place and leaps again over the counter, coming to rest beside* GLAS. GLAS *sits, slowly, on the stool*)

ROSIE   (*Upon seeing the gun*)   Randall! (RANDALL *puts on his glasses. He puts the muzzle of the gun to* GLAS's *temple.* ROSIE *screams*) Randaaal!
   (*She moves as though to leap from the counter, but* RANDALL *wheels and turns the gun at her; she freezes*)

RANDALL   (*Quietly*)   Sshh. (ROSIE *is wide-eyed, transfixed.* GLAS *is motionless.* RANDALL *again places the muzzle of the revolver against* GLAS's *temple; he pulls the trigger and the hammer falls, audibly, on the empty chamber. Silence*) Done, then . . . You got a short span of memory, little chick. It empty, you recall? (*He places the*

gun at her breast and pulls the trigger: another click)
You recall now? *(He places the muzzle at his own tem-*
ple, pulls the trigger. Then again, pointing it this time,
but not touching, GLAS's head and again pulls the trigger.
He gazes at GLAS. Pause) It's done, Rosie.
    (Pause. ROSIE is badly shaken)

ROSIE   *What's* done?

RANDALL *(With a shrug)* Something. *(Turning to her,*
breaking away from his attention on GLAS) You know:
the *something* you spoke of?
    (He slowly pulls the wig from his head)

ROSIE   You almost scared me to death, you bastard, you
nut!

RANDALL   Well, it make as much sense as *some* trials I
could mention.
    (GLAS moves, finally. He rises from the stool and
    speaks without looking at RANDALL)

GLAS   It should have been loaded, hah, Randall?
    (Pause)

RANDALL   No sword of justice will pierce *your* heart, Mister Glas.
    (He drops the gun on the counter)

ROSIE   I think it's time I left this madhouse.
    (She makes no move, however)

GLAS   Do you understand, Rosie?

ROSIE   No. But it doesn't really matter whether I do or
not, does it? All I know is I'm very depressed. *(She picks*

up the gun. On her face there appears a look of disturbance, puzzlement) Randall . . .

RANDALL   Hm?

ROSIE   You didn't really know, did you.

RANDALL   Know what, little Rosie?

ROSIE   About the gun. I mean, you didn't really know it wasn't loaded.

RANDALL   Sure I did, Rosie. Didn't he say so?

ROSIE   But you didn't really *know*. He might not have been telling you the truth when he said it wasn't loaded. You didn't look to see, or anything. It *could* have been loaded. You didn't really *know*.
     (Pause)

RANDALL   You asking a lot of questions, Rosie, without the answers to match.

ROSIE   It's true, isn't it.

RANDALL   What's true?

ROSIE   That you didn't really know. Suppose it *had* been? Suppose it *had* been loaded?

RANDALL   Well, then, that woulda been another contingency which we woulda—

ROSIE   *(Thrusting the revolver beneath his eyes)* Suppose it had been *loaded*, Randall! *(Pause.* RANDALL *merely gazes at her, inscrutably.* ROSIE *is terrified at the possibilities, the implications. Her eyes well with tears)* I don't understand.

RANDALL Well, it's a clock shop, little Rosie, we're all telling a different time. (*Turns to* GLAS) Isn't that right, Mister Glas?

GLAS That's right, Randall.

ROSIE Did you hear what he said?

GLAS Whatever he says, that's right. (*To* RANDALL) You know, Randall. (*To* ROSIE) He *knows*.

ROSIE What does he know?
(GLAS *sits at the counter, staring out the window, his back to them, and remains so*)

GLAS Tell Rosie what you know, Randall.

ROSIE (*Hysterically*) But, Mister Glas! He didn't *know*! (*Brandishing the gun*) He didn't *know* it wasn't loaded. He could've *killed* you! You could be *dead*! Don't you understand!

GLAS (*Calmly*) Of course, I understand, Rosie.

ROSIE Well, *I* don't. I really don't.
(*She weeps*)

GLAS (*Without turning*) Rosie, Rosie . . .

ROSIE I think you're *both* crazy, that's what I think. I thought it was only him, but it's you too.

GLAS I knew it wasn't loaded, Rosie.

ROSIE But, *he* didn't, goddamnit! *He* didn't know! Why won't you listen! He could've been killing you, for all he knew!

GLAS He was, Rosie, he was. Sshh. Don't cry. (*She is unconsolable*) Randall, tell her you knew it wasn't loaded.

RANDALL (*Readily*) I knew it wasn't loaded.

ROSIE You're lying! You're lying!

GLAS Sshh. It doesn't matter, Rosie, it doesn't matter.

ROSIE Of course, it matters! *Jesus Christ!*

GLAS Not to me, Rosie. Not to Randall.

ROSIE (*Screaming*) It matters to me!

RANDALL Why, Rosie?

ROSIE *I don't know!*

RANDALL You seem overly concerned with the condition of knowing and not knowing, Rosie. The state of knowing is entirely in the realm of—

ROSIE Oh, shut up, shut up, shut up, shut up!

GLAS Rosie ...
    (*Pause. She begins to calm*)

RANDALL (*As to a child*) Rosie ... what Mister Glas means when he says it doesn't matter ... what he means is you didn't even know he existed before a couple of hours ago, right? Up till a couple of hours ago you didn't know such a man as Mister Glas was present on the face of the earth, right? And, moments from now you'll pass again through that door and thoughts of him will occupy your mind for what will amount to no more than a fragment of all the time of your life and he will become only one more of the many lost memories. Because that's the way it is, little Rosie, that's the way it is.

ROSIE (*Violently*)   That's *not* the way it is!

RANDALL (*Regretfully, commiserating*)   And I thought you had no illusions, Rosie.

GLAS   Leave her alone. (*In his attempts at consolation* GLAS *has remained with his back to* ROSIE. *He turns, now, for the first time*) Forget it now, Rosie.
(*Pause*)

ROSIE (*Quietly, resigned*)   No . . . I won't forget it . . .

GLAS   Won't they be missing you at home, Rosie?

ROSIE   No.

RANDALL   I should think they'd be missing you at home at this late hour, Rosie.

ROSIE   I'm supposed to be staying with a friend tonight.

RANDALL   Ah.
(ROSIE *is despondent now; her "front" is gone, her responses are dead and flat*)

ROSIE   I didn't want to go home—after the doctor. So I told them I'd be staying at a friend's. Now I'll have to go through the whole thing all over again, all the arrangements and everything.

RANDALL   You're really going to do that thing, then, hah, Rosie?

ROSIE   Of course I'm going to do it. Why not.

RANDALL   Ah. (*Pause*) Well, it'll be a new experience for you, Rosie, you'll be able to put it in one of those books you're going to write.

ROSIE   That's not very funny.

RANDALL   Everything is fuel for the flame, Rosie.

ROSIE   What flame.

RANDALL   The flame of creation! *You* know! The creation of Art! It's very interesting, actually. The substitution of the false for the real, the counterfeit for the genuine, the phony for the real McCoy. Very interesting, actually. Take yourself, Rosie. I mean, you have yourself a *real* creation blooming away like a little flower there in your belly only you're going to have it chopped out some evening this week and then someday you'll probably re-create the whole experience all over again except it will be merely words on paper then for someone to pass the time away with. (*His attitude changes suddenly to one of quiet intensity*) Rosie . . . don't do it, Rosie.

ROSIE   What? (*Pause*) What do you mean, don't do it? (*Pause*)

RANDALL   (*Breezily again*)   Nothing.

ROSIE   What's it to you, anyway?

RANDALL   (*In the dialect*)   Ain't nothin' ta me, little chick, nothin' atall.

ROSIE   It's easy for you to say, isn't it. Don't do it. Just like that, don't do it.

126

RANDALL We don't have to pursue the matter, Rosie, if you don't care to.
(*Pause. She studies him*)

ROSIE You're judging *me* now, aren't you. Like *him*.
(*She points at* GLAS, *who is silent, motionless*)

RANDALL Not at all, Rosie. I understand.

ROSIE What do you mean, you understand? How would you? You ever been knocked-up?

RANDALL Not to my knowledge.

ROSIE All right, then.

RANDALL It's merely a convenient phrase, Rosie: I understand. *You* know, a manner of—communication—not to be taken literally.

ROSIE You think I *want* to do it?

RANDALL That's a very tricky question, Rosie, I decline to answer. I'm told we do what we most want to do.

ROSIE Well, of course, I *want* to. But I don't *really* want to. I have no choice.

RANDALL Of course.

ROSIE I *don't*.

RANDALL (*With sudden violence*) You *do*!
(*Pause*)

ROSIE (*Quietly*) But not one that I care to take.

RANDALL Ah. Ah, yes. Yes, yes, yes. Did you hear, Mister Glas?

127

GLAS Yes.

ROSIE I have to do it. (*Pause*) You understand, don't you, Randall? Mister Glas?

RANDALL What does it matter whether or not we understand, Rosie?
(*Pause*)

ROSIE (*With all the "front" at her command and for what is probably the last time in her life*) That's right! What does it matter! It happens every day, right? And I have no patience with all the whispered-behind-the-hand hypocrisy about the facts of life, however *sordid* . . . (*Then quietly, quickly*) . . . they may sometimes be.
(*Pause*)

RANDALL You angry with me, Rosie?

ROSIE What do you care?

RANDALL But I do.

ROSIE Why.

RANDALL Because you're such a truly splendid chick. The most splendid I ever knew.
(*Pause*)

ROSIE No, I'm not angry with you. A little frightened of you, maybe.

RANDALL Why frightened, Rosie?

ROSIE Because you confuse me. I have to know who people are or else I become confused and I tend to be frightened by things that confuse me. I don't think *you* even know who you are, Randall. I don't think you even *think* you know who you are.

RANDALL Think, Rosie? *Think?* I know not *think.* You know that saying, "I think, therefore I am?" (ROSIE *waits*) You know who said that, I suppose? (ROSIE *waits*) It's a bunch of *bosh,* baby. I *feel,* therefore I am: *that's* the truth.

ROSIE What do you feel, Randall?

RANDALL Oh, many things.

ROSIE Easy answer, Randall. What things?

RANDALL Private things.

ROSIE Phony.

RANDALL Hm?

ROSIE You! *"Private things."* Bullshit, Randall! Phony!

RANDALL (*Seizing her*) Not phony! Not! Not! You want to know what I feel? You want to *know?* There is a *passion* loose in the world! A passion for the sounds of violence, for the sight of pain! A passion for death and disaster! We're up to the eyeballs in blood, little chick: you gotta swim in it or drown in it, one or the other. Listen! You hear that? You hear that long, faint, faraway roar out there? You gotta listen good and you'll hear it. Listen! Hear it? You know what that is? That's the yahoos screaming for blood out there! Isn't that right, Mister Glas!

GLAS (*Without turning*) That's right, Randall.

RANDALL It's a butcher shop, little Rosie! *Where's your cleaver!*

ROSIE I'll never take up a cleaver.

RANDALL Then you gotta be fast on your feet, little chick! Fast, *fast* on your feet! (*He releases her. Then, more quietly*) Unless you want to be like Mister Glas and bury yourself in a hole and wait for someone to come along and execute you with an imaginary bullet in the brain. That's also a way. But, ever which way, it all comes to the same thing in the end, Rosie: no hiding place.

ROSIE From what, Randall.

RANDALL From what?

GLAS (*Without turning*) Tell us, Randall. It's time.

RANDALL Is it? Is it that time already?

GLAS You owe it to us, Randall.

RANDALL Do I. (GLAS *nods*) Yes, I suppose I do, all things considered, mm, hm. (*Pause*) It's my mother, you see . . . You recall my mother, Mister Glas . . . (*Pause. He begins to go off into a dreamlike state*) Oh, Mother, Mother . . .
(*Pause*)

GLAS Go on, Randall.
(*Pause*)

RANDALL Up the stairs, first. One flight, two flights, three flights, four. Through the door. Into the room. Dark. Sit. Wait. Noises in the bedroom, familiar noises in the

bedroom. Creak, moan. Creak, moan. Creak, moan. Momma moaning, giving value for money. Wait. Quiet. Dark. Clock, tickticktick, clock, tickticktick. Fire engine. Clock, tickticktick. He comes out of the bedroom, head down, faceless man, buttoning, shoelaces clicking on the linoleum. Out the door. Slam. Quiet. Wait. Bedspring creaks. Match strikes in the bedroom. Exhalation. Don't smoke in bed, Momma: everybody says. Randall stands up. Into the bedroom. Momma on the bed, black on white. Screams. Covers up. No words. Screams when the knife comes down. Screams when the knife comes down. Screams when the knife comes down. Many times. Knife breaks. Ice pick. Small round holes in the white sheet pumping blood. No screams . . . No screams no more . . . no momma no more, no momma no more . . .
 (*Pause*)

ROSIE   Ohmygod . . . ohmygod . . . Mister Glas, he . . .

GLAS   I heard, Rosie.

ROSIE   Oh, Randall . . . Why!
 (*She weeps*)

RANDALL   A long story, Rosie, and you came in late.

ROSIE   Ohmygod . . .

RANDALL   Do you know the Cloisters, Rosie?

ROSIE   They'll catch you, Randall, they'll kill you!

RANDALL   That's a quiet place, the Cloisters, like where them monks used to live long ago. I sure woulda liked to be one a them monks. Maybe next time.

ROSIE   Oh, Randall, Randall, there won't be any next time! They'll kill you for what you've done!

RANDALL   Of course, but I mean after that. The next time I come back. I neglected to tell you, Rosie, you see, I believe in the Resurrection and the Life—in the truest sense. Surely, this isn't the only crack we get at it? Surely not. How absurd that would be. So, I figure maybe next time I be a monk . . . and live in a quiet place . . .
   (*Pause. He puts on his hat*)

ROSIE   What are you going to do, Randall?

RANDALL   Time to go, Rosie.
   (*He takes up the umbrella*)

ROSIE (*Desperately*)   Maybe they won't catch you, Randall! That's right! How will they know it was you!

RANDALL (*Smiling*)   Your thinking on it seems to be somewhat confused, little Rosie. I have broken the laws of God and Man, you're supposed to want to see me apprehended and brought before the bar of justice and be delivered up to mine executioners.

ROSIE (*Still weeping*)   I don't care what I'm *supposed* to want.

RANDALL   "She lov'd me for the dangers I had pass'd. And I lov'd her that she did pity them . . ." You know who said that? (*No response from* ROSIE) Anyway, a couple of people saw me, you know? Who know me. Also, the knife, that's still there, my fingerprints firmly impressed upon the handle.
   (ROSIE's *body is convulsed with a shudder*)

ROSIE God, God ...

RANDALL Do you believe in Hell, Rosie? That's the one thing worries me a bit, that I might go to Hell. Of course, you must understand, my conception of Hell is not that of others, the Eternal Flames and all. There are no flames involved in Hell. What Hell really is is the denial of rebirth. The soul is a ghost, adrift. Adrift, and aware of life, looking for a new body to inhabit, a new flesh, looking for a way back into the world, into life. And being denied it. That's Hell, little chick. No flames involved. No flames atall.

GLAS Randall. (RANDALL *turns to* GLAS. GLAS *points at* RANDALL *but does not look at him*) "Which way I flie is Hell; myself am Hell."

RANDALL *Very good*, Mister Glas, sir! Who said that?

GLAS (*Shrugs, shakes his head*) Someone.

RANDALL Ah. (*He turns again to* ROSIE) And Heaven, Rosie—Heaven is that first filling of the lungs with that first breath of a new life.

ROSIE Mister Glas! Can't we *do* something?

RANDALL (*Grinning*) There you go again, Rosie. Tell her, Mister Glas.

GLAS (*His back to her*) Don't you see, Rosie ... Randall must die now, violently, because of what he is and because of what he has done. And I will *live*, without violence, because of what I am and what I have done. And you, Rosie ... you will go to your doctor, up that dark street, and afterward ... you will write books,

133

maybe . . . about how people should save each other . . .
We choose, Rosie. We choose the dark streets up which
we walk. We choose them. And if we are guilty of the
denial of life . . . who is there to save us from that . . .
but ourselves?

(*Pause. She looks at* GLAS, *at* RANDALL)

ROSIE   *God damn it!*
(*She turns away. Pause*)

RANDALL   A splendid chick, don't you think, Mister Glas?
(GLAS *nods*)

GLAS   Are you going to make them look for you, Randall?

RANDALL   Yeah, I think I'll give 'em a little bit of a run
for their money. You know me.

GLAS   Yes.

RANDALL   Of course, when they catch up with me, though,
that'll have to be the end of the story, I'll have to make
sure of that. The other alternatives are—unthinkable.

ROSIE (*Covering her ears*)   Don't talk like that, Randall!

RANDALL (*To* GLAS, *ignoring her*)   To be locked in a
white, silent room or to be fried in my own juice. The
one would be a bore, the other a bit melodramatic for
my taste. So this'll have to be the end of this particular
time around.

GLAS   That will be the best way, yes.

RANDALL   So I guess I better get crackin'.

134

GLAS   Good luck, then, hah, Randall?
        (RANDALL *moves to the door, opens it, and stands*
        there looking out, his back to GLAS *and* ROSIE)

RANDALL   Man! man! I sure don't like it out there.
        (ROSIE *turns away*)

GLAS   Randall . . . maybe next time . . . Maybe next time,
        a quiet place.
        (*Silence.* GLAS *takes a candle from the box still on*
        the counter, a remnant of the never-completed in-
        ventory. He holds the candle in his hand a moment,
        then strikes a match and lights the wick. He drops
        a bit of melted wax on the counter-top and fastens
        the candle to it. He gazes into the flame. All three
        are back to back now)

                    Curtain

About the Author

William Hanley was born in Lorain, Ohio, in 1931 but has lived most of his life in and around New York City. He began writing plays in 1957. His first produced work, two one-act plays, *Whisper into My Good Ear* and *Mrs. Dally Has a Lover*, were presented off-Broadway in 1962 and were the recipients of a Vernon Rice Award. His play *Conversations in the Dark* is scheduled for Broadway production in the near future and he is presently at work on a new play. Mr. Hanley is married, has one child, a daughter, and lives in New York City.

DATE DUE

MAR 6 '68			